CHRISTMAS IN THE WHITE HOUSE

CHRISTMAS
IN THE WHITE HOUSE

Albert J. Menendez

THE WESTMINSTER PRESS

PHILADELPHIA

Portions of Frederick M. Feiker's letter to his daughter Janet are used by permission of W. Feiker.

Excerpts from *My Memoir*, copyright © 1938, 1939, by Edith Bolling Wilson, are used by the courtesy of the publisher The Bobbs-Merrill Company, Inc.

PICTURE CREDITS: Associated Press, pp. 34, 96; Bill Fitz-Patrick, the White House, p. 120; The Free Library of Philadelphia, pp. 62, 71; *Harper's Weekly*, pp. 31, 59, 77, 79; The Lyndon Baines Johnson Library, pp. 50, 118; *Frank Leslie's Illustrated Weekly Newspaper*, pp. 14, 60, 69, 89, 105; Mount Vernon Ladies' Association of the Union, p. 11; *St. Nicholas Magazine*, p. 25; Harry S. Truman Library, pp. 100 *(top)*, 114; White House Photo, pp. 16, 27, 37, 42, 53, 73, 100, 101.

BOOK DESIGN BY DOROTHY ALDEN SMITH

First edition

Published by The Westminster Press ®
Philadelphia, Pennsylvania

PRINTED IN THE UNITED STATES OF AMERICA
9 8 7 6 5 4 3 2 1

Library of Congress Cataloging in Publication Data

Menendez, Albert J.
    Christmas in the White House.

    Bibliography: p.
    1. Presidents—United States. 2. Christmas—United States. I. Title.
E176.1.M463 1983   973'.09'92   83-3629
ISBN 0-664-21392-8

Contents

Introduction   7

1
It's an Old Family Custom   9

2
Men and Women of Good Will   23

3
The Pitter-Patter of Little Feet   29

4
O Christmas Tree!   39

5
Parties   55

6
Gifts   67

7
Feasting   76

8
Romance   87

9
Going Away for Christmas   92

10
A Greeting from the President   *102*

11
A Quiet Christmas   *104*

12
The President Speaks   *111*

Bibliography   *125*

Introduction

Christmas at the White House means many things. It means a sparkling Thomas Jefferson playing his fiddle for young people, a tearful Andrew Jackson telling orphans about his own horrible childhood, a jovial Franklin D. Roosevelt reading Dickens' *A Christmas Carol* to the family, and a stern Theodore Roosevelt forbidding Christmas trees in the White House. It also means a Christmas wedding and honeymoon for Woodrow Wilson, the first lighting of a National Christmas Tree by Calvin Coolidge, and a surprise dinner for poor children hosted by Abraham Lincoln's son Tad. And much more.

These and many other human interest stories associated with the warmest and happiest time of the year are included in this volume. What makes it special is that all are true, and that the characters are those special men and women whom history anointed the First Families of the United States.

A wide array of sources has been used in putting together this little excursion into social history: diaries, published and unpublished memoirs, letters, reminiscences of White House staff, biographies and autobiographies of Presidents, First Ladies, and the children of the Presidents. Files of newspapers and library archives have been assiduously searched. Presidential libraries have been helpful, as has the Office of the Curator at the White House. As always, I am grateful for the help and support of my wife, Shirley, to whom I dedicate this book.

So let us begin by turning back the pages of history and peering behind the wreaths of evergreen and holly at number 1600 Pennsylvania Avenue.

1

It's an Old Family Custom

Part of the joy of Christmas is the repetition of familiar customs and traditions, often handed down from one generation to another. Some family customs of Presidents were dictated, to a large extent, by the shared values of their community or region. This was especially true of the early Virginia Presidents: George Washington, Thomas Jefferson, James Madison, and James Monroe.

George Washington always kept Christmas with an abundance of joy and merrymaking. As a Virginia gentleman, he welcomed visitors and friends to his plantation with open arms. The food was sumptuous, the decorations tasteful, the fire crackling, and the conversation animated.

Eighteenth-century Virginians took their holiday celebrations seriously. Their English heritage and Anglican faith had much to do with their favorable view of the season. Historian Julian P. Boyd wrote: "Living in this mild climate and fair land, Virginians celebrated the season with joyful abandon, making the days from Christmas Eve to Twelfth Night reflect their own particular character and ways. The period of lusty eating, drinking, entertaining, and good fellowship that characterized Christmas in the drafty baronial halls of feudal England had much in common with that in Tidewater Virginia."

Merrymaking was a strenuous activity. The festivities lasted for a month or more. Boyd continued: "The boar's head and the peacock of Christmas in the baronial halls of England had given way to the wild turkey and the venison of the Virginia plantations. But the feasting and merriment had the same lusty quality. By day the men pitched quoits, rode to the hounds, hunted, raced, or fought their gamecocks, with occasional spells of quiet for courting, talk of politics, or business matters involving the purchase of land, the selling of slaves, or the swapping of blooded horses. By night there was much feasting, singing, dancing, carousing, and gaming, with more and more-intensified courting. Such diversions as cards, dice, backgammon, and chess were available for those who fancied them, while 'Blind-Man's Bluff,' 'Hoop and Hide,' 'Hunt the Slipper,' 'Break the Pope's Neck,' and other games of forfeit involving much random kissing and laughter were no doubt universal favorites with men and women alike. Such festivities prevailed throughout the season, with only occasional pauses to revive drooping spirits."

Washington loved Mount Vernon, and Jefferson cherished Monticello. Both tried to be "home for Christmas." When circumstances intervened, they were homesick.

In 1776, on Christmas night, Washington crossed the Delaware River, a scene immortalized in poetry, picture, and song. In 1777, he and his valiant men spent a frigid, depressing holiday at Valley Forge. There was no milk, eggs, flour, tea, coffee. No pastries or pies. No spirits or traditional grog. The wretched soldiers had only cabbage, turnips, potatoes, and a bit of fowl.

But later Christmases were once again happy. On the twenty-third of December, 1783, Washington's resignation of his commission as Commander-in-Chief was tendered to Congress, then convening at Annapolis, Maryland. The war had ended after Yorktown. Washington returned to his beloved Mount Vernon on Christmas Eve. Family, friends, and servants greeted the conquering hero with rousing cheers, song, pistol shots, and firecrackers.

We have limited information about Washington's Christmases as President. The President's residence was in New York, and it can be assumed that the Washingtons yearned for Mount Vernon.

In 1789, the President and the First Lady attended morning services at St. Paul's Church in lower Manhattan and received visitors in the afternoon. The President commented that his Christmas Day visitors "were not numerous but respectable."

After his retirement, the general liked to write letters on Christmas Day, this being several decades before the sending of Christmas cards.

The Father of his Country died shortly before Christmas in 1799. Henry Lee delivered his now-famous funeral oration before Congress on December 26, concluding: "First in war, first in peace, and first in the hearts of his countrymen, he was second to

10

Washington loved Mount Vernon
and tried to be "home for Christmas"

none in the humble and endearing scenes of private life."

Teddy Roosevelt once said, "There is something about Christmas that is almost indescribable." Even the eloquent and well-read Mr. Roosevelt was awestruck at the mystery and solemnity of Christmas. One thing he insisted upon was the continuity of family traditions.

The Roosevelts loved to pile into their sleighs (and later their motorcars) and drive to Oyster Bay for the Christmas Eve carol service. The Roosevelt family pew in Christ Church was always filled. The Roosevelts made family reunions of Christmas, and their festivities always commenced at the carol service.

Theodore Roosevelt usually gave a brief ad-libbed sermonette. Consequently, he could not remember his subject title from year to year and often repeated his remarks. The rector, Mr. Talmadge, told him one year, "Colonel, you tell that story better each time."

Sometimes Mr. Roosevelt tended to be a bit lengthy in his addresses. One Christmas Eve, he was greeted by fierce whispers from his children as he rose to walk to the pulpit. "Father, don't speak long. Think of the poor children," they said.

11

The little village church was brightly lighted with candles and draped in green. To the left of the pulpit stood the Christmas tree, resplendent in gilt and tinsel. Oranges, nuts, candy, and a great pile of presents lay in the chancel. Gifts were distributed to all the children after services ended.

The closing hymn, "Christmas on the Sea," was the carol Teddy Roosevelt loved best. It is an indigenous carol, sung only at Christ Church at Oyster Bay to this day. It appears in no hymnals or songbooks. Teddy Roosevelt said: "We have adopted it for our own. Where it came from none of us know, but it came a long time ago, for we have been singing it at our Church for a couple of hundred years. It was evidently used when Oyster Bay was a whaling village and the menfolk put forth on long cruises around the Horn and into the Pacific."

Burl Ives recorded this jaunty air in 1972, on a record called *Christmas at the White House.* Here are the words to this lovely carol:

CHRISTMAS ON THE SEA

It is Christmas Day by the river
It is Christmas Day by the bay
And the soft winged snows
They are falling
On the ocean far away.

From the hands of God
They are falling.
Snowy doves on this Christmas Day.
On the havened waves of the river
On the ocean far away.

There are happy lights by the river.
There are happy lights by the bay.
And the lonely lights
They are drifting
O'er the ocean far away.

But the sailor thinks of his dear ones
And his home on this Christmas Day.
While the wind sweeps
Wild through the cordage
On the ocean far away.

Now the bells ring over the river
Now the bells ring over the bay.
But the ships still move
In the silence
O'er the oceans far away.

But the sailor's heart, it is cheery
And he says, "It is Christmas Day."
And though the winds and waves
May be dreary
They are happy far away.

Roosevelt bought armloads of presents for his large family. Usually each child had a whole table of presents in the drawing room for his or her own delight. Stockings were filled. Mr. and Mrs. Roosevelt often included a special poem for each child on certain of their presents. Teddy Roosevelt delighted in the "rustling of paper and excited exclamations as each gift [was] pulled out."

Promptly at 8 A.M. on Christmas Day, the gift-opening ritual began. Roosevelt explained: "For some time before this the children have been up. The patter of their feet and muffled exclamations have made us lamentably aware of the fact that sleep was over and we were delaying proceedings."

Roosevelt continued his description: "Soon the room becomes a maelstrom of paper and gifts, and looks as if some giant had emptied his scrap basket in it. In one chair a child is sitting cross-legged reading a book. On the floor another, with trembling fingers, is putting together a mechanical train. In the corner a third is trying out a new flashlight, endeavoring to create sufficient darkness by hunching his coat over his head.

"Then the household come in for their presents, which are given to them by the children. By this time it is noon and we all gather at Sagamore Hill for lunch, where Mother presides over a long table, lined on both sides with her children and grandchildren. The youngest are put by their mothers, the eldest, as less important, are by their fathers. Great platters of food are brought in. There is a whole roast pig with an apple in its mouth. This year my youngest wanted to know why the apple? There is cider in tall pitchers. Finally comes a plum pudding, burning bravely. The boys eat an appalling amount. Their appetites would shame the fat boy in *Pickwick Papers*."

A Thomas Nast cartoon of 1901, "Happy Santa Claus at the White House," celebrates Teddy Roosevelt's delight in the children's Christmas

The remainder of the day was spent in playing out of doors, singing carols, or listening to Roosevelt tell Christmas stories by the big tree in the North Room.

Strangely enough, Woodrow Wilson preferred to play golf or attend the theater on Christmas. He rarely attended church on that day, though his second wife, Edith Bolling, insisted on going to St. Margaret's or St. John's Church for Communion.

There was always a nice Christmas breakfast, followed by gift-opening by the fire. In 1917, the family went to Keith's Theatre. Then they returned to the White House for a gala dinner for twenty—another Wilson tradition. After dinner everyone played charades.

14

Mrs. Calvin Coolidge loved music. It was her idea that carols should be sung on the North Portico (the front porch, in effect) of the White House in 1923, her first Christmas as First Lady. Sixty-five vested choristers from the First Congregational Church sang that Christmas, while the public was admitted to the grounds to listen. The President and son John joined the singing. The minister of the Coolidges' church, Dr. Pierce, had composed a hymn, "Christmas Bells," which he dedicated to the First Lady. It was sung that night. The singers were accompanied by a pianist and three trumpeters from the U.S. Marine Band. This custom was continued all during the Coolidge years, but the Hoovers discontinued it.

Grace Coolidge also delighted in adding an old-fashioned New England touch to the White House decorations. The windows were decorated with laurel wreaths tied with bright-red bows. Over the front doorway was hung a huge wreath with red berries and pinecones, lighted at night with tiny colored electric lights. In the first year of her husband's presidency, there were two Christmas trees, a large one in the Blue Room and a smaller one in the upstairs room that her sons occupied. In the following years, the south end of the East Room was set aside for a miniature nativity scene. This was placed on a slightly raised platform, covered with green carpeting and surrounded by potted ferns. The background was composed of five evergreens. The topmost peak of the large middle tree held a silver star illuminated by a tiny electric light. In the shadow of these trees stood a small stable with a thatched roof. Inside in a manger lay the figure of the Christ-child, lighted by the rays of an electric light.

Mrs. Coolidge loved the nativity crèche. She once wrote, "From this quiet corner the real spirit of Christmas seemed to radiate to every recess of that old mansion and beyond."

President Coolidge insisted on rising early on Christmas, usually before 7 A.M. He dressed and then took a morning stroll through the rear grounds and ellipse area, which he called "the south lot." He insisted that an early-morning walk improved his appetite for breakfast.

The rest of the day was spent in opening gifts, attending church, dining, and taking a "Christmas nap."

Mrs. Herbert Hoover's favorite custom was to extinguish all lights in the White House. Then her friends and family would march from room to room, carrying lighted candles and singing

The Franklin Roosevelt clan gathers
for the 1937 festivities

carols. Before becoming President, Mr. Hoover loved to gather his
own tree and greens.

The Franklin Roosevelts loved Christmas so much that their
infectious spirit was inevitably communicated to the whole household. A kind of electric excitement buzzed through the old mansion as December lengthened and the days shortened.

Commented Henrietta Nesbitt, the housekeeper and cook
whom the Roosevelts brought from Hyde Park to the White
House: "When Christmas came, all the five-ring-circus excitement
of the past year seemed to gather to a point in the White House
and explode in a lather of tinsel stars. I never saw so much excitement and so much affection shown. I never knew people that
loved Christmas the way the Roosevelts did.

"That was the spirit that came out strongest at Christmastime. The President felt the same way, so everyone around the
Roosevelts felt their happiness, and there never was a Christmas
in the White House while they were there that wasn't joyous."

White House seamstress and maid Lillian Rogers Parks felt

16

the same way. She wrote in the wonderfully informative *My Thirty Years Backstairs at the White House:* "Christmas time was the best time to be at the White House. I have never seen a person more excited by the holiday season than Mrs. Roosevelt."

Mrs. Roosevelt tried to explain some years later how she had managed to survive a White House Christmas. She wrote: "When Christmas is spent outside one's own home, particularly in government surroundings such as the White House, you divide your Christmas in two parts. One covers your official obligations; the other, as far as possible, is the preservation of the home atmosphere and the home routine."

Franklin and Eleanor Roosevelt both loved "the smell of hot evergreens." They insisted on having real candles on real trees, because, Mrs. Roosevelt said, "a tree doesn't look right without real candles and does not give the right atmosphere unless it smells of hot evergreen."

So the Roosevelt family tree on the second floor of the White House—and at Hyde Park—always had real lighted candles. The local fire department and the Insurance Underwriters Association both warned against the practice. The tree in the East Room had electric lights. In 1934, the White House announced that the trees would be treated with a fireproof solution to prevent a possible tragedy. (In 1921, the Warren Hardings announced their intention of having lighted candles, but relented when the insurance men protested. The poor Hardings. Everything they planned to do at Christmas went amiss. In 1922, they canceled a holiday excursion to Pinehurst, North Carolina, because of Mrs. Harding's sudden illness.)

The Roosevelts made Christmas a warm, imaginative, and rich occasion. The decorations, the food, and the atmosphere were impeccably traditional. Another FDR custom was the President's reading of Charles Dickens' *A Christmas Carol* to the family on Christmas Eve after dinner. The President loved this classic depiction of repentance and reformation of character. He knew whole sections by heart. He gave each character in the novel his best interpretation.

Elliott Roosevelt remembered that last Christmas in 1944: "The center table in the long living room was pushed back, the Christmas tree was in place and decorated, the piles of presents were ready for the unwrapping—each person's pile heaped on a separate chair. And on Christmas Eve, Father took his accustomed

17

rocker, to one side of the fireplace, and opened the familiar book, while we all found places around him. My place was prone on the floor, by the grate. The fire crackled pleasantly; Father's voice, going over the well-remembered *Christmas Carol*, rose and fell rhythmically; my thoughts wandered, aimless, and presently ceased altogether. Then, Jab!, in my ribs came Faye's elbow, and her fierce whisper in my ear: 'You were snoring! Sit up!' and I looked up sheepishly at Father, who only winked at me gravely, and went on reading."

At that same reading, another poignant incident took place. Jim Bishop described it this way: "Mr. Roosevelt began a solemn and highly dramatic reading of Dickens' *Christmas Carol*. Head back to take advantage of his bi-focals, he simulated the inoffensive, frightened voice of Bob Cratchit and the menacing snarl of Mr. Scrooge. About at the halfway point a three-year-old grandson noticed a tooth gap in the lower part of the President's mouth. He pointed excitedly and shouted, 'Grandpere, you've lost a tooth!' Mr. Roosevelt allowed himself a brief smile and returned to the story. The little boy stood to get a better look and said, 'Did you swallow it?' The President slammed the book shut and fell into a paroxysm of laughter. He had to wipe his eyes. He glanced at the adults in the far reaches of the library. 'There's too much competition in this family for reading aloud,' he said. Faye Emerson said, 'Next year, it will be a peaceful Christmas.' Eleanor Roosevelt nodded seriously. 'Next year,' she said, 'we'll *all* be home again.' "

The Franklin Roosevelts also enjoyed a quiet Christmas breakfast, attending church on Christmas Eve or Christmas Day (usually at St. Thomas' in Washington), and movies after dinner on Christmas Day in the evening.

FDR's favorite carol was an unusual one: "Art Thou Weary, Art Thou Laden?" Sometimes called an Epiphany hymn, it is listed as a general hymn in the Episcopal hymnal, which Roosevelt would have used. It has a fascinating history. It was written by Stephen the Sabaite, an eighth-century Greek who spent eighty years as a monk in Mar Saba Monastery, five hundred feet above a canyon floor in the rocky wastelands of Judea, ten miles south of Jerusalem. The hymn lay dormant for a thousand years, until a nineteenth-century Anglican priest, John Mason Neale, discovered it in Constantinople. Neale's life interest was the translation of thousands of hymns of the Greek and Latin fathers into English. Thanks to his work, Western Christians today sing such beautiful hymns as "All Glory, Laud, and Honor," "O Come, O Come, Emmanuel," "Come, Ye Faithful, Raise the Strain," and "Jerusalem the Golden."

The text for "Art Thou Weary, Art Thou Laden?" is taken from the words of Jesus as recorded in Matthew 11:28: "Come unto me, all ye that labor and are heavy laden, and I will give you rest."

Here is the hymn that FDR loved so well:

> Art thou weary, art thou laden,
>   Art thou sore distrest?
> "Come to me," saith One, "and coming,
>   Be at rest."
>
> Hath he marks to lead me to him,
>   If he be my guide?
> In his feet and hands are wound-prints,
>   And his side.
>
> Is there diadem, as monarch,
>   That his brow adorns?
> Yea, a crown, in very surety,
>   But of thorns.
>
> If I still hold closely to him,
>   What hath he at last?
> Sorrow vanquished, labor ended,
>   Jordan past.
>
> If I ask him to receive me,
>   Will he say me nay?
> Not till earth, and not till heaven
>   Pass away.
>
> Finding, following, keeping, struggling,
>   Is he sure to bless?
> Saints, apostles, prophets, martyrs,
>   Answer, "Yes."

Dwight Eisenhower and Thomas Jefferson both loved "O Come, All Ye Faithful"; Ulysses S. Grant preferred "O Little Town of Bethlehem"; and Abraham Lincoln enjoyed "We Three Kings of Orient Are." Zachary Taylor's favorite carol was "It Came Upon the Midnight Clear." Lyndon and Lady Bird Johnson claimed "Silent Night" as their favorite. George Washington liked "While

19

Shepherds Watched Their Flocks by Night"; John Adams liked "Joy to the World!"; and Andrew Jackson enjoyed an American hymn "Shout the Glad Tidings." This last hymn, now forgotten, was written by an Episcopal clergyman, William Augustus Mühlenberg, and given its premiere at historic Trinity Church in New York City on Christmas Day 1826.

Dave Powers, a special assistant to President John F. Kennedy, recalled that the President asked a strolling band at a White House staff party to play "Silver Bells," a popular modern American carol.

President and Mrs. Harry S. Truman enjoyed a real family Christmas. Their daughter, Margaret, said, "Dad would have walked through the drifts to get home to Independence for Christmas." He even flew in dreadful weather. Once his plane just made it to the airport before a severe snowstorm. The press plane got caught in it, and arrived late.

On Christmas night, "since time immemorial," the Trumans went to Uncle George and Aunt Beuf's house for "leftovers." Aunt Beuf's leftovers consisted of "whole baked hams, cold turkeys, mounds of jellied salads and savories, pies, cakes, and homemade ice cream."

Alas, it was not always possible to go home for Christmas, and the White House Christmases were never quite so festive, though Mr. Truman carved the turkey himself in 1947. The Trumans were always thoughtful of their staff. After the 2 P.M. dinner, Bess Truman asked to have the third-floor kitchen supplied with sandwiches for supper so that the staff could go home to their families for the remainder of the day.

The Eisenhowers wanted nothing more than to be with their son and grandchildren. They sang carols around the family Christmas tree on the second floor. In 1955, Mamie played the organ. They distributed the gifts on Christmas Day. The family always attended services at the National Presbyterian Church.

Mamie loved trees and decorations. It was often said that the White House never looked nicer than in the years the Eisenhowers lived there. Every window had a green wreath tipped by a red bow. There were trees everywhere—twenty-six of them at one Christmas. A large nativity scene was placed in the East Room. Mrs. Eisenhower added a loudspeaker that poured forth carols. In 1960, she added a three-foot-high Santa Claus in red-velvet costume to the collection beneath the tree.

20

In 1959, Mamie subbed for Ike at all the Christmas parties. The President was then on his goodwill mission abroad and returned just before Christmas. In the State Dining Room, the center of the table contained a miniature train, its open cars filled with tiny packages. Even the wall lights were tied with red ribbons. The room was ablaze with carnations and holly.

In Palm Beach, Florida, the Kennedy family trimmed a floor-to-ceiling tree on Christmas Eve and hung stockings from the mantel. Silver and gold angels graced the mantelpiece.

At the entrance to the Kennedy home on the Atlantic Ocean was a two-feet-high white Santa Claus. The main entranceway was lined with tall poinsettia plants. The centerpiece for the Christmas dinner was Santa Claus riding in a sleigh pulled by two reindeer.

Mrs. Lyndon Johnson took a great interest in seeing that Christmas was just right. "Christmases for us," she wrote, "have been touched by the continuity of tradition and the mood of the time."

One Johnson custom was "the annual honor show," the gathering of relatives for a picture-taking session. Most of them were in no mood for having their pictures taken. President Johnson preferred to take the photographs himself. Mrs. Johnson also remembered Christmas as being a time of "laughter, children, bedlam, crash shopping expeditions and frantic last-minute activity."

Lady Bird Johnson was an innovator. She briefly restored the Coolidge custom of singing Christmas carols, though she used the South Portico. This was in 1965, when West German Chancellor Ludwig Erhard came for a state visit. The American Light Opera Company Chorus sang carols in his honor. Lady Bird also placed the family Christmas tree in their favorite room—the Yellow Oval Room on the second floor.

It is to Lady Bird Johnson that the White House owes the magnificent eighteenth-century crèche. The First Lady asked Mrs. Charles W. Engelhard, Jr., to find an appropriate crèche for the White House Christmas collection. She went all over Europe before finding twenty-two Neapolitan figures from the eighteenth century. It was an acquisition commensurate with other White House art treasures.

The figures range from twelve to eighteen inches high. They are made of wood, with hands and faces delicately carved in the Italian baroque manner. All are richly clothed, and the three wise

21

men are riding horses rather than camels.

Mrs. Engelhard obtained the crèche through the Christmas Crib Association of Italy. The association sent her to Signora Marisa Piccoli Castello of Naples, whose family had been collecting crèche figures for over three hundred years. Signora Castello could speak no English and was reluctant to part with her figures. The crèche was given its premiere, in an exquisite setting of blue velvet studded with stars and angels, on December 13, 1967.

Lady Bird also cherished heirloom Christmas decorations, which she generally kept at the ranch. For, as she put it, "one of the great joys of Christmas to me is bringing out the treasured old things seasoned with warmth, like the stockings an old-time Texas friend embroidered for us when Luci was a year old. Here at the White House, Christmas is more impersonal, but I enjoy the perfection of it in a different way."

2
Men and Women of Good Will

Doing for others, placing the needs of others above oneself, is the essence of the Christmas spirit. Throughout this book we will see the caring and compassion of our presidential families for their own families, relatives, and staff. But this caring and compassion have also extended to perfect strangers.

Andrew Jackson had a special feeling in his heart for orphans. One year he visited the orphan asylum, carrying a carriage full of packages and sweets. When he was asked about Santa Claus, the President became pensive and rather sad-faced. He responded, "I once knew a little boy who not only never heard of Christmas or Santa Claus but never had a toy in his life; and after the death of his mother, a pure, saintly woman, had neither home nor friends." Then he choked up, his eyes brimming with tears, and left the room. He had been describing his own childhood.

Having regained his composure, the President distributed gifts to the orphans. He gave a jumping jack to a delighted crippled boy, who cried: "Ain't that cute? Hopping up and down just like an organ grinder's monkey."

Upon leaving, the President told the matron, Mrs. Van Ness: "The best way to secure happiness is to bestow it on others, and we'll begin our holiday by remembering the little ones who have no mothers or fathers to brighten life for them."

Abraham Lincoln's son Tad had a warm and thoughtful heart. On Christmas Eve in 1863, Tad came to see his father, who was still working at his desk. He had received an armful of books from his parents, but he told his father he wanted to send them to soldiers. "Do you remember how lonesome the men looked?" Tad asked, for he had accompanied his father on visits to military camps. Mr. Lincoln thought for a moment, with a gleam in his eye, and answered: "Yes, my son, send a big box. Ask Mother for plenty of warm things, and tell Daniel to pack in all the good eatables he can, and let him mark the box 'From Tad Lincoln.' "

On Christmas Day, 1864, Tad encountered a band of ragged street urchins outside the White House. They had no place to go for Christmas dinner. Tad invited them into the White House kitchen, but the cook refused to feed them and tried to have them expelled. Tad went to his father, who was greeting some important guests at the front door. "Of course they may come in," the President replied and ordered the cook to give them all turkey dinners. It is said that his face lighted up with a rare smile, for his son Tad knew how to keep Christmas.

Mrs. Ulysses S. Grant always tried to remember the unfortunate. In her biography *The General's Wife,* Ishbel Ross writes: "At Christmas the asylums, hospitals, and orphanages received generous donations from the Grants, often in the form of barrels of fruit and confections. Toy merchants and jewelers counted on Mrs. Grant's bounty, for she bought freely for the young and frequently led a parade of unidentified children through the shops, making them happy with her gifts."

In 1883, four children's Christmas Clubs were formed in Washington, D.C., for the purpose of feeding needy youngsters. Adult ladies and gentlemen volunteered to help the young people. President of the District II Club was Miss Nellie Arthur, small daughter of President Chester A. Arthur. Plants and evergreens from the White House decorated the hall and "from the same old mansion came the Small President of the Club escorting the Big President of the Republic" as her guest. Five hundred children were feted and feasted.

In 1914, Woodrow Wilson granted Christmas pardons to two federal prisoners so that they might spend the holidays with their families. Four years later, on Christmas Eve, he commuted the death sentences imposed by a military court on two deserters. Each year Mr. and Mrs. Wilson distributed presents to children who greeted the First Couple on their way to the Washington Country Club in Arlington, Virginia. It was an annual custom that

Needy guests hurry to the Christmas feast
of the Children's Christmas Club

the Wilsons enjoyed. But the gift list increased from seventeen to nearly a hundred in their last year. The President was so busy in 1917 that Mrs. Wilson and Rear Admiral Cary T. Grayson, the President's physician, distributed the gifts.

In 1926, Grace Coolidge gave a dance for sixty boys and insisted on doing a turn with each of them. She also distributed gifts at Salvation Army headquarters, cheered the veterans at Walter Reed Hospital, sent sixty poinsettias to her church, and shared in a public greeting to all the children of the United States. In 1928, President Coolidge issued the first executive order giving federal employees in Washington a holiday on December 24. Before that time Christmas Eve was not a holiday.

Lou Hoover always visited the Central Mission to bestow presents, and Eleanor Roosevelt went into the slums on Christmas Day to deliver food and gifts to the needy. The visits had quite an effect on Mrs. Roosevelt. She once wrote: "Christmas afternoon, I always made the rounds of Christmas trees in the Alleys. The Alleys were slums of Washington, and a group would set up sad little trees, around which children would gather for presents. It would be arranged that I would drop in on each little group as they collected. From these gatherings, I always went back to the White House with an added awareness of the inequality of our earthly blessings."

In 1945, President Harry Truman asked his staff to find two needy families so that he could provide Christmas for them.

In *My Twenty-One Years in the White House,* Alonzo Fields tells this story: "I shall always remember the first Truman Christmas in 1945. About a week before, the President said one morning when he was alone at breakfast, 'Fields, I should like to request a favor. I want you to find a needy colored family and see to it that they have a real happy Christmas dinner. I have already asked Dressler (the agent in charge of the Secret Service detail to the President) to find a needy white family.'

"The President went on to say that he did not want it known. He took out his purse and gave me some money, saying, 'This is to buy each child in the family a present. If this isn't enough, let me know.' "

This became an annual custom for President Truman at Thanksgiving and Christmas.

In 1953, President Dwight Eisenhower sent "bushels of toys" to Faith Home in Danville, Virginia. The story of the way

Grace Coolidge surrounded by friends
from the First Congregational Church, 1923

this came about is quite unusual.

Mrs. Clay Daniel, a retired public school teacher, received Faith Home's annual appeal in November. Faith Home was an institution for orphans or children who were unwanted. Each potential donor received a card bearing the likeness of one of the children. Mrs. Daniel felt that one little boy looked remarkably like the President. So she sent the photograph and an explanation of the campaign to the President. That is why seventy-three children received a bundle of toys from the President of the United States.

In 1955, Mr. Eisenhower granted Christmas pardons to forty-two persons convicted of federal offenses and commuted a condemned murderer's sentence. One of the recipients of this presi-

27

dential clemency had been in prison since 1898. Also in 1955, Mrs. Eisenhower sent a personal Christmas greeting to a ninety-four-year-old former slave, David Townsend, who operated the greenhouse at the officers' club at Fort Meade, Maryland. The Eisenhowers had been stationed at Fort Meade in 1919 and 1920.

Mrs. John F. Kennedy played Santa Claus at the District of Columbia Children's Hospital, in 1961, presenting gifts to two hundred patients. She told the staff, "I don't know when I've been more touched."

Twenty years later, Mrs. Ronald Reagan visited the same facility. It was from the hospital's yellow wing that the First Lady called the family of Katie Beckett in Cedar Rapids, Iowa. The Reagans had intervened to let the little three-and-a-half-year-old girl go home for Christmas. Because of current Medicaid rules, the girl had spent most of her short life in a hospital. The family would have lost Medicaid benefits if Katie had been treated at home. The First Family also sent a doll to the little Iowa girl.

3
The Pitter-Patter of Little Feet

Christmas is for children. How often that sentiment has echoed down through the centuries. But then, Christmas is, after all, the story of the divine Child of Bethlehem.

Children have enlivened presidential Christmas celebrations since Christmas Day in the year 1800, when John and Abigail Adams hosted a party in a frigid White House. (Frigid because the numerous fireplaces just couldn't keep the drafty old mansion warm.) The entire dwelling was cold, damp, and unfinished. Abigail complained, "Not a chamber is finished of a whole."

To make the place bearable for their first Christmas, she burned twenty cords of wood in each of the fireplaces, in an attempt to dry the plaster. Shortly before the children's party, members of Congress and their wives arrived for a reception. One account says that the First Lady was "distressed and embarrassed because it was still cold. The guests sat around trying to look comfortable and hide their gooseflesh, but they left early."

The children's party, however, seemed warmer if only because of its uninhibited joviality.

Susanna, the four-year-old orphan of President Adams' son Charles, was the only child resident at the new executive mansion. (It was not really called the White House until Teddy Roosevelt's Administration. It was, in fact, brownish in color. After the burning by the British in 1814, it was painted white.) Susanna received from Santa Claus a beautiful set of dishes for her dolls, but an envious playmate at the Christmas Day party smashed them. In retaliation, spirited Susanna bit the nose and cheeks right off her playmate's new wax doll. Pandemonium followed, and President Adams himself had to quiet the guests and soothe the injured feelings.

In 1805 widower Thomas Jefferson invited all six of his grand-children to the White House and threw an enormous Christmas party for them. Dolly Madison, whose husband was then the Secretary of State, served as hostess to the one hundred children who trampled through the President's House. Jefferson was so caught up in the Christmas spirit that he grabbed his violin and played some zesty tunes for his guests. They danced and cheered, and the scholarly President continued playing for hours.

One year the seven children at the Jackson White House brought tears of joy to the old general's face. They hung a stocking over the fireplace in their Uncle Andrew's room, telling him that Santa would certainly not forget the President! During the night they sneaked down and filled the stocking "heap full of trinkets." Early the next morning the President's secretary found him weeping over the gifts, for, as a child, he had never received a Christmas gift.

An unforgettable party occurred in 1835. Children all over Washington received this invitation: "The children of President Jackson's family request you to join them on Christmas Day, at four o'clock P.M., in a frolic in the East Room." And a frolic it was.

The White House was filled with childish glee and chatter. The President's famous French chef, Vivart, created his awesome ices and confections. There was laughter and dancing and unrestrained game-playing, at which even the staid vice-president, Martin Van Buren, joined in.

The President's private secretary, Major Donelson, had four children who lived at the White House with the two children of Jackson's adopted son. Sixty-five years later, one of them, Mary Donelson Wilcox, published her memory of this wonderful Christmas party. Here is her remembrance of the supper:

"About six o'clock the dining room was opened, displaying a picture of surpassing beauty, one that the four seasons and field, forest, and lake had united in embellishing. The band stationed in the corridor struck up the 'President's March,' and Miss Cora, forming us in line, the younger couples leading, marshaled us into supper. The scene of many historic banquets, commemorating great events and shared by world-wide celebrities, that famous room never witnessed one in which the decorator's art, or the confectioner's skill, achieved greater triumphs—Vivart, hailed as Napoleon of Cooks, Master Chef de Cuisine, Wizard, Magician, receiving hearty congratulations on all sides. In the center of a maltese-cross-shaped table towered a pyramid of snow-balls, interspersed with colored icicles and surmounted by a gilt game cock, head erect, wings outspread. At the upright ends of the cross were dishes of frozen marvels, at the top one representing iced fruits—oranges, apples, pears, peaches, grapes; at the bottom one

A joyous family Christmas was depicted in Harper's Weekly *December 30, 1865, but the White House was still saddened by the loss of Willie Lincoln*

representing iced vegetables—corn, carrots, beans, squashes. At one transverse end was a tiny frosted pine tree, beneath which huddled a group of toy animals; at the other a miniature reindeer stood in a plateau of water in which disported a number of goldfish. There were candies, cakes, confections of every conceivable design; delicious viands, relishes and beverages. Though almost transfixed with admiring delight, we did ample justice to the tempting repast and eagerly accepted the lovely ornaments given us as souvenirs."

After supper the children were delighted with the artificial snowballs, made of noncombustible starch-coated cotton. Since the winter had been mild that year, the children had been deprived of their usual snowballing games. So for a few minutes the East Room was the scene of a dazzling blizzard. But as all good

31

things come to an end, it was time to go.

The children bowed and kissed the President's hand, saying, "Good night, General." He smiled and bowed in return. Dolly Madison, present as always at White House social functions, said to the President, "What a beautiful sight. It reminds me of the fairy procession in *A Midsummer Night's Dream.*" The President thought a moment and responded, "It recalls to me, Madam, our Divine Master's words: 'Suffer the little children to come unto me and forbid them not, for of such is the Kingdom of Heaven.'"

For the Lincolns, Christmas meant being with their three sons. Nothing else—war, intolerable burdens, or public abuse—could detract from the family togetherness in 1861. Bob (Robert Todd) was home from Harvard. Willie celebrated his eleventh birthday on December 21, and Tad was a free-spirited eight-year-old. Looking back several years later, Mary Lincoln wrote of that Christmas, "We were having so much bliss."

But Willie died in February 1862, and the remaining Lincoln Christmases were never the same. One incident involving Tad is worth retelling. In her *Lincoln's Sons,* Ruth Painter Randall tells this story:

"Just before Christmas when Mr. Lincoln was conferring with a member of his Cabinet, Tad burst into the room like a bombshell sobbing and crying with grief and a sense of outrage. The turkey was about to be killed for the Christmas dinner. Tad had managed to procure a stay of execution while he flew to lay the case before his father. Jack must not be killed, he sobbed, that would be wicked.

"'But,' said the President, 'Jack was sent here to be killed and eaten for this very Christmas.'

"'I can't help it,' cried Tad passionately. 'He's a good turkey, and I don't want him killed.' Mr. Lincoln reached for a card and wrote out a formal reprieve for Jack. Tad seized it joyfully and fled to set his pet at liberty. From that time on, Jack became a character on the White House grounds."

Christmases with the Rutherford B. Hayes and the Benjamin Harrison families were totally given over to children. A Washington newspaper account of Christmas in 1890 said bluntly, "The children took possession of the Mansion for the day." The Harrisons' grandchildren were delighted with their presents—a new tricycle and a blue dress and the "gorgeously decorated" tree in the Library.

32

The Grover Clevelands' last Christmas in 1896 was an especially happy one. Their three daughters were now at an age to appreciate the holiday. A carnival was held in the library for the three little Cleveland girls and the children of Cabinet members. A fir tree, decorated with tinsel, gilt, and artificial snow, stood in the center of the room, its top touching the ceiling. The bright-eyed children cavorted around it, and, after refreshments, little Ruth and Esther Cleveland, who had been learning German, gave recitations. This was followed by the telling of Christmas stories and the singing of carols by the children.

Another party was held with the children of the President's executive secretary, Daniel Lamont. The President supervised the hanging of stockings on the chimney shelf. "A whole room was filled," says one account, "to its utmost capacity with wonderful gifts and toys."

Theodore Roosevelt loved to buy gifts for his brood of children. In one of his delightful letters, he asked, "I wonder whether there ever can come in life a thrill of greater exaltation and rapture than that which comes to one between the ages of say six and fourteen, when the library door is thrown open and you walk in to see all the gifts, like a materialized fairy land, arrayed on your special table?"

In a letter to Master James A. Garfield, the President told how he celebrated Christmas in 1902:

"Yesterday morning at a quarter of seven all the children were up and dressed and began to hammer at the door of their mother's and my room, in which their six stockings, all bulging out with queer angles and rotundities, were hanging from the fireplace. So their mother and I got up, shut the window, lit the fire, taking down the stockings, of course, put on our wrappers and prepared to admit the children. But first there was a surprise for me, also for their good mother, for Archie had a little Christmas tree of his own which he had rigged up with the help of one of the carpenters in a big closet; and we all had to look at the tree and each of us got a present off of it. There was also one present each for Jack the dog, Tom Quartz the kitten, and Algonquin the pony, whom Archie would no more think of neglecting than I would neglect his brothers and sisters."

The following year he wrote this description to his sister Mrs. Douglas Robinson: "We had a delightful Christmas yesterday—just such a Christmas thirty or forty years ago we used to have

The Hoover grandchildren deliver party invitations

under Father's and Mother's supervision in 20th street and 57th street. At seven all the children came in to open the big, bulgy stockings in our bed; Kermit's terrier, Allan, a most friendly little dog, adding to the children's delight by occupying the middle of the bed. From Alice to Quentin, each child was absorbed in his or her stocking, and Edith certainly managed to get the most wonderful stocking toys. Bob was in looking on, and Aunt Emily, of course. Then, after breakfast, we all formed up and went into the library, where bigger toys were on separate tables for the children."

On another Christmas Eve, Edith Roosevelt invited six hundred children of officials in her husband's Administration to a festive fete at the White House. "Instructions were sent out that adults could accompany only the most timid of the children, and the nurses were kept downstairs while the party was in progress," is the way one observer described the evening.

Following the party, a popular musical group sang in the East

Room. Then a rich feast was held in the State Dining Room. The President helped to serve the creamed oysters and other delectables to the happily assembled youngsters.

In 1929, the Hoovers' grandchildren, Peggy Ann and Peter, were the center of attention at the Christmas celebration. A special table was set for them, so they could dine with the fifty adult guests on Christmas Eve. Afterward they led the guests on a candlelight tour through the darkened White House, singing carols and ringing bells.

The next Christmas, the Hoovers invited a group of young people to a party, the purpose of which was to gather gifts for needy children. The invitations read like this:

Mrs. Hoover
and
Peggy Ann and Peter
request the pleasure of the company of
Miss Mary Alice Shaw
and
Master David Edward Shaw
on Wednesday, December twenty-third
from half after three to five o'clock

THE WHITE HOUSE
WASHINGTON

This is not like the Christmas parties you usually go to, where you get lots of toys and presents to take home, and *very* many good things to eat.

But it is a party where you bring toys and warm gay sweaters or candy, or things other children would like who otherwise would not have much Christmas.

For Santa Claus has sent word that he is not going to be able, by himself, to take care of all the little boys and girls he wants to this year, and he has asked other people to help him as much as possible.

So if you bring some presents with you, we will send them all to him to distribute. And we will send most of the candy and "snappers" and cake and "such" to him, too!

The party was a rousing success. The decorations were magnificent. The U.S. Marine Band played carols and hymns. Food, gifts, and storytelling made the time pass. Each child received a present, horns, whistles, and other favors. Mrs. Hoover insisted on marching the children through the White House, upstairs and down, to the accompaniment of the band. As darkness settled over the house, a group of Girl Scouts, carrying glowing lanterns, sang the yuletide songs of old.

Grandchildren were important to the Eisenhowers too. "Now our Christmas starts," smiled Mrs. Eisenhower as the President carried his one-year-old granddaughter, Mary Jean, into the White House on Christmas Day in 1956. (The child had been born the previous Christmas.)

In 1961, four-year-old Caroline Kennedy tried to sneak an early peek at the White House Christmas tree, but she was detoured by order of her father. Holding his hand, she stepped off the elevator that carried them from the family living quarters to the first floor. Then she broke away and dashed toward the closed doors of the Blue Room, where workmen were putting the finishing touches on a huge balsam fir patterned after the "Nutcracker" tree. "Not now, Caroline, later," the President said, grabbing her arm. Like children everywhere, little Caroline could hardly wait to see the family tree.

Mrs. Kennedy began a now-annual tradition of entertaining poor children at the White House in 1961.

By 1968, the Johnsons were giving several parties for Washington area children. First came a party for underprivileged children from Washington's "Junior Village." For this event, the operetta *The Wizard of Oz* was performed on the East Room stage by the Washington Civic Opera Association. The Cowardly Lion was the hit.

Then came a party for the children of diplomats assigned to the national capital. An hour-long film, *Dr. Coppelius,* was shown.

Santa Claus, played by Sanford Fox of the White House invitations office, was mobbed at both parties. The children ran after him from the dining room to the entrance hall, where they grabbed gifts in scenes reminiscent of a bargain basement sale.

In 1981, Nancy Reagan gave a party for 178 hearing-impaired children. They came from the Kendall School, the federally funded elementary school at Washington's Gallaudet College for the deaf. Mrs. Reagan secured the talents of Virl and Tom Os-

*Grandchildren were the focus of the
Eisenhower Christmas*

mond, of the famous Osmond family, and the dancer Jacques
d'Amboise, who directs the National Dance Institute in New York
City, which conducts a special dance class for hearing-impaired
children.

Mrs. Reagan was a wonderful hostess. She had learned the
sign language for "I love you," and the feelings were mutual. She
was quite a hit with the youngsters. One little girl hung on to her
hand the whole time.

The Osmond brothers, who are themselves hearing-impaired,
did a top hat and cane dance, and then played Christmas carols on
the saxophone, piano, Swiss bells, and xylophone. Most of the audience joined in the singing of "We Wish You a Merry Christmas."

37

Local actors volunteered their time and wore flamboyant costumes designed by Henri Bendel. There was a chef with an onion necklace, a queen with a castle on her head, a blackbird, a dove, a lady in a tricorn hat, and two mimes in ruffles and skullcaps, who did tricks with their faces.

Everyone was served cider and cookies, and each child received a present from the First Lady. Each one also received a calico elephant or angel.

As President Ronald Reagan said in his 1981 Christmas message: "Christmas means so much because of one special child. But Christmas also reminds us that all children are special, that they are gifts from God, gifts beyond price that mean more than any presents money can buy. In their love and laughter, in our hopes for their future, lies the true meaning of Christmas."

4

O Christmas Tree!

When the President of the United States lights the National Christmas Tree this year, he will be continuing a grand tradition.

The Christmas tree is part and parcel of almost every American home today. But it was not always so. What Charles Dickens once called "that pretty little German toy" did not become a well-established feature on the American Christmas landscape until the 1840's. Holly and evergreens sufficed before Americans discovered and adopted an ornament long beloved by the German people, the decorated tree. This was true at the President's House.

It was a sad and lonely President, Franklin Pierce, who first erected a small tree in the White House in 1853. He invited the Sunday school class of the New York Avenue Presbyterian Church to join him and the First Lady for a celebration of the holiday. The Pierces were still in mourning for their son, Benny, the victim of a railway accident shortly before the inauguration. But President Pierce insisted on making the occasion bright and cheery for his visitors.

The Lincolns, the Grants, and the Hayeses all enjoyed Christmas trees, so much so that Benjamin Harrison could refer to the custom as "old-fashioned." Edna Coleman, in her chatty account of the human side of the presidency, described the Harrisons' 1889 Christmas tree: "A very large, gorgeous tree was put up in the library, in the trimming of which the President, his family and the staff assisted. It carried toys not only for the children of the family but for everyone attached to the White House and their families. Around it, too, were piled the hundreds of gifts and remembrances sent by friends and presidential admirers."

An ardent conservationist, Teddy Roosevelt initially forbade any tree at the White House. But his children were so disappointed and public opinion so hostile that he gradually relented. One year Roosevelt's son Kermit disobeyed his father's orders and placed a tree in his private quarters on the second floor. He decorated it himself and stocked it with presents. The President's heart was touched, and he no longer prohibited a tree. His friend and fellow conservationist Gifford Pinchot convinced him that cutting the trees down would not drive them into extinction.

The year 1923 saw the inauguration of a custom that has taken on national significance and has lasted until today: the lighting of the National Community Christmas Tree by the President. Calvin Coolidge began this delightful ceremony, but it was not he who originated it. Mr. Frederick M. Feiker, an adviser to Herbert Hoover, suggested that the President light a Christmas tree on behalf of all Americans and in recognition of the spiritual significance of Christmas.

In a letter to his daughter, dated March 8, 1932, Feiker tells how it all began. "The Society for Electrical Development was interested to have as many people use electric lights at Christmas time as possible, so I thought of this idea of having the National Christmas Tree at Washington, which would stimulate other people to have outdoor Christmas trees. In order to get this started, we had to get the President of the United States to light the tree. If you can get the President of the United States two years in succession to do a thing, he will always do it. The first year, I arranged to have Mr. Coolidge, who was President, presented with a tree from Vermont. Middlebury College donated the tree. It was shipped by express by the alumni of the College, and set up in Washington by a committee formed of the various local organizations, which I also arranged. We collected about $5,000 from the electrical industry to install the underground lighting cables to the spot behind the White House where the tree was erected.

"I went with the Senator from Vermont to see Mr. Coolidge, and secured his agreement to light the tree. We got the National Broadcasting Company to broadcast the ceremony. Mr. Coolidge refused to speak, but he did agree to push the button."

In a related ceremony, carols were sung from the North Portico of the White House. The precursor of this custom occurred in 1916, when Mr. and Mrs. Woodrow Wilson walked across the street to the Treasury Building to hear carols sung. The Wilsons' appearance was unexpected, but it may have been prompted by the fact that the President's daughter Margaret was the soloist.

Neither event received much attention from press or public.

The National Christmas Tree has had a hard time finding a permanent home. It remained in Sherman Square, which is just east of East Executive Drive, from 1924 to 1933. Then it was moved to Lafayette Park, on the north side of the White House, from 1934 to 1938. It went back to the Ellipse in 1939 and 1940. But Mrs. FDR liked the South Lawn of the White House, so she could feel "close" to the people. It was erected there from 1941 to 1953. Finally, in 1954 it returned to the Ellipse, then called The President's Park, where it has remained ever since.

There were some sound reasons for all this moving. In 1934, E Street was enlarged, necessitating a reshaping of Sherman Square. There was not enough space to accommodate the growing crowds that came to the ceremony. In 1941, the Secret Service wanted to minimize risks to the President's life and thought that holding the event on the White House lawn would make their job easier. Some Secret Service officials wanted to cancel the ceremony for the duration of World War II, but the Christmas-loving Chief Executive vetoed that suggestion.

In 1924, the ceremony was again held on Christmas Eve. The tree was a large Norway spruce, and it was lighted with electric candles.

The tree-lighting ceremony was almost canceled, however, after only one year. In early 1924, President Coolidge made a statement to the American Forestry Association against cutting trees for Christmas. (Shades of Teddy Roosevelt!) Fred Feiker was aghast when he heard the news. He told his wife that the lovely new Christmas custom would not survive. She immediately retorted, "Why not plant a living Christmas tree?" So they did.

Will Hays, then chairman of the Republican National Committee and later the morality czar in Hollywood, was also chairman of the Amawalk nurseries. Hays arranged to send a living tree to be planted on Sherman Square. Then the President consented to light it. So the dour Mr. Coolidge did not let down the growing crowds who now looked forward to the annual ceremony.

The next year, the crowds were larger, an amplifier was erected, and the ceremony was broadcast nationwide by NBC. At 6 P.M. President Coolidge touched the button that illuminated the "Great Yule Tree." As the lights came on, hundreds of motorists blew their horns. Then all was silent while the U.S. Marine Band played hymns and carols for a full hour. Inside the White House,

the Coolidges erected three trees of their own. One was decorated
with Mrs. Coolidge's "lucky" white ivory elephants.

In 1927, the crowds were larger than ever. A coronet soloist
played "Cantique de Noel" (also called "O Holy Night"), a haunt-
ing melody that remained on the annual program into the 1960s.
The tree had five hundred lights and two thousand reflecting
jewels. Trumpets played, horns blared, and church bells rang.
Later that evening a choir from the Interstate Commerce Commission sang carols.

The following year the festivities were held at 8 P.M., which
added a romantic quality. Most of the scene was in darkness.
Lights shone only on the stage from which the President spoke.
Fully four thousand Washingtonians and tourists surrounded the
tree and collected on the steps of the Treasury Building.

As the tree was suffused in a blaze of glowing colors, Boy Scout
buglers signaled the beginning of Christmas Eve. Arthur S. Wit-
comb gave his usual stirring coronet solo of "O Holy Night," and
the U.S. Marine Band played some then-popular melodies, such as
"Christmas Echoes" and "Bells Across the Snow." Before the presidential party departed, a Boy Scout presented to Mrs. Coolidge
a large engraved card, which declared that she "had always been
gracious and had won the hearts of the people of Washington." It
was a golden evening, that last Coolidge Christmas in an era of
prosperity.

Nothing very eventful took place during the four times the
Hoovers presided over the ceremonies. In 1929, fifty Washington
school children serenaded the President. In 1931, Pepco, the local
electric company, took over the electrification process. In the
Hoovers' last year a "Singing Christmas Tree" was featured. That
year, also, a group of positive-spirited Washingtonians called upon
the citizenry to sing carols as a way of fighting the Depression and
the spirit of gloom that pervaded the country. Handbills blanketed
the city.

In 1933, the National Capital Parks Office took over all ar-
rangements for planting and caring for the tree. For several years
they used trees planted in Lafayette Park. Then they decided to

43

transplant a tree each year from the Mount Vernon Parkway. It was returned to its homesite on New Year's Day.

The crowds increased during the Franklin Roosevelt years. The President was immensely popular, particularly in Washington. In 1935, glass stars shone like diamonds from the tree. New platforms, candles, and an eight-sided fence were added in 1936.

The next year two hundred Christmas trees were placed in the city's poor neighborhoods, to be illuminated at the same time that the President pushed the button in Lafayette Park on Christmas Eve. Mrs. Roosevelt played a role in the citywide activities preceding the main event.

The tree of 1938 was called a "dream of beauty" because of magnificent new lighting donated by the Electric Institute of Washington. Mercury vapor floodlights added a new dimension and quality to the illumination. Kresge's Department Store donated ornaments and chimes.

The following year a soaking rain drenched the 2,500 hardy souls who braved the elements and watched the ceremonies in person. One hundred and sixty radio stations carried the event.

President Roosevelt told the crowds in 1940 that he was hoping to move the ceremony to the White House lawn the following year so that he could wish all Americans a Merry Christmas from his own house. Of course, Mrs. Roosevelt and the Secret Service also had something to do with that decision.

The years of World War II brought about some changes in the annual event. The ceremonies were now on the White House South Lawn. The Secret Service screened all the people who were admitted. Tickets were hard to come by, and there were reserved seat stands for the fortunate few.

Britain's valiant Prime Minister Winston Churchill was quite a hit during his surprise appearance in 1941. Churchill had secretly traveled across the Atlantic for an important war council with President Roosevelt. It was so secretive, in fact, that FDR did not tell Eleanor until Christmas Eve that Mr. Churchill and his party would be arriving that day!

That Christmas was overshadowed by the horrible events abroad, which had inexorably drawn the United States into a world war against the Axis Powers. Pearl Harbor was a very recent memory. Most of Europe groaned under the swastika. For millions of American families, the fear of deprivation and wartime dislocations, of death to loved ones, was now ever-present.

The war spirit had pervaded the White House. Air-raid shelters were being dug on the White House lawn, and heavily armed soldiers paraded endlessly through the grounds. Police and Secret Service agents stood watch. Important officials came and went. America was again at war.

But it was still Christmas, and Christmas was part of what we were fighting for. Mr. Roosevelt welcomed a crowd of thousands who had been admitted to the White House grounds for the annual Christmas Eve lighting of the National Christmas Tree. Mr. Churchill was at his side. The crowd seemed more reverent, more attentive, than in years past. The message was broadcast to the nation. Mr. Roosevelt said, in part, "Against enemies who preach the principles of hate and practice them, we set our faith in human love and in God's care for us and all men everywhere."

The Prime Minister then made a brief statement. He said: "Let the children have their night of fun and laughter. By our sacrifice and daring, these same children shall not be robbed of their inheritance, or denied the right to live in a free and decent world."

Along with the crowd the two leaders of the Allied Forces then sang Christmas carols and the two national anthems.

On Christmas Day, the President took Mr. Churchill to worship services at Foundry Methodist Church. Though both were Episcopalians, Mr. Roosevelt told his Secretary of Labor, Frances Perkins, that he wanted the Prime Minister "to hear some good-old Methodist hymn-singing" because no one, he thought, sang hymns so lustily as the Methodists.

The President also issued a proclamation making New Year's Day "a day of prayer, of asking forgiveness for our shortcomings of the past, of consecration to the tasks of the present, of asking God's help in days to come."

On New Year's Day, the Prime Minister was again the President's guest for worship services, this time at Old Christ Church in Alexandria, Virginia, the Episcopal parish where George Washington often worshiped. They sat together in Washington's pew.

Mr. Roosevelt issued a statement on the national day of prayer that said, in part: "We are confident in our devotion to our country, in our love of freedom, in our inheritance of courage. But our strength, as the strength of all men everywhere, is of greater avail as God upholds us.

"We need his guidance that this people may be humble in

45

spirit but strong in the conviction of the right, steadfast to endure sacrifices and brave to achieve a victory of liberty and peace."

Later in the day, Roosevelt and Churchill went to Mount Vernon, George Washington's beautiful estate on the Potomac. It was raining, but the house was dressed in Christmas finery. Standing beside a red-brick tomb, Mr. Churchill bared his head and placed a red, white, and blue wreath on the grave of our first President.

For security reasons the tree was unlighted in 1942 and 1943. Ornaments were donated by various service clubs around the country. A tag on each ornament listed the name of a U.S. fighting man overseas, a touching remembrance from the folks back home. Some ornaments included photographs of a loved one, a son, brother, or husband, fighting on some faraway battlefield.

By 1945, when Harry Truman first presided, the ceremony was carefully orchestrated. Each minute was accounted for. The program looked like this:

THE LIGHTING
OF THE
NATIONAL COMMUNITY CHRISTMAS TREE, 1945

THE WHITE HOUSE LAWN

Monday, December 24, 1945, at 4:30 P.M.

Timed Program

4:30–4:57	Marine Band Concert	27 minutes
4:57–5:00	Carols by Washington Choral Society	3 minutes
5:00–5:03	Arrival of the President and his party........	3 minutes
5:03–5:05	Invocation—Rt. Rev. Mons. Thos. G. Smyth...	2 minutes
5:05–5:08	Introductory Remarks, Brig. Gen. Gordon R. Young, National Chairman.............	3 minutes
5:08–5:11	Greetings to the President and Mrs. Truman, by Boy and Girl Scouts	3 minutes
5:11–5:15	Carols....................................	4 minutes
5:15–5:16	Lighting of the Tree by the President........	1 minute
5:16–5:22	President's Christmas Greeting to the Nation .	6 minutes
5:22–5:24	"Cantique de Noel", Cornet Solo	2 minutes
5:24–5:26	Carol.....................................	2 minutes
5:26–5:27	Benediction—Rev. Dr. C. W. Cranford.......	1 minute
5:27–5:28:30	The National Anthem	1½ minutes

46

But the Trumans showed little interest in the event. The President wanted to be home in Independence, Missouri, on Christmas Eve and did not even appear at the 1948, 1949, and 1951 ceremonies.

An article in *The Washington Post* for January 9, 1952, was headlined, "Yule Absence of President Is Deplored." Miss Sibyl Baker, assistant superintendent of the District of Columbia Recreation Board, urged that efforts be made to "rehabilitate the Community Christmas Tree." She said it was "regrettable that the custom of having the President light the tree has about disappeared."

Genuine fears were expressed that the nearly thirty-year-old tradition would be ended. For when the President did not appear, the crowds dwindled. Miss Baker's records showed that attendance had been seriously affected by the President's absence. Would the event die?

The Christmas ceremony received a one-year reprieve when Dwight Eisenhower became President. The tree-lighting was held on the White House lawn in 1953, but the large and friendly crowds were forced to remain behind the iron fence. Only a lucky few received permission to view the events close up. Much criticism was voiced.

But a new lease on life occurred in 1954. An entire restructuring of the annual tree-lighting ceremony was effected. For one thing, the date was pushed back to December 17. For another, the site was the much more spacious Ellipse, called The President's Park in those days. Finally, the event was renamed "The Christmas Pageant of Peace." Ceremonies lasted until January 6, Epiphany or Twelfth Night, the traditional ending of the Christmas season.

The changes were felicitous. Linking the tree-lighting to the yearning of the American people for peace created much more attention nationwide. The event began to take on great symbolic significance. It was now televised nationally.

The organizers were animated by a positive principle. They said: "The Pageant of Peace is a voluntary expression of American citizens of every creed and race to dramatize the Christmas Message 'Peace on Earth, Good Will Toward Men.' It is organized to foster friendship and understanding among all peoples; to reflect the unity of purpose that emanates from the diversity of traditions and backgrounds of mankind."

President Eisenhower was warmly supportive. He encouraged the efforts and looked forward to his participation each year. Twenty-two nations and twenty-seven states and territories donated small trees to grace the Pathway of Peace, which flanked the walkway leading to the gigantic National Community Christmas Tree. The large tree was donated by the State of Michigan.

The decorations were typical of America of the 1950s. Mr. Leonard Johnson of Smethport, Pennsylvania, loaned the Pageant of Peace Citizens Committee a life-size Santa Claus, eight reindeer, and an electrically operated Christmas display.

The ceremony became more elaborate each year. Citizens groups were involved in planning the many activities that surrounded it throughout much of December and early January. The organizers even set up a permanent office and a nonprofit corporation, called the Christmas Pageant of Peace, at 1616 K Street in the heart of downtown Washington.

In 1957, a gas-powered sleigh manned by Santa Claus carried children on rides near the great tree, a 60-foot gift from Minnesota. The Voice of America carried the ceremony overseas.

Bigger and better seemed the bywords. Now every state donated a small tree for the Pathway of Peace. A life-sized nativity scene, floodlighted at night, was set up in 1954 and remained a popular attraction until a law suit concerning "establishment of religion" necessitated its removal in 1973.

Back at the White House, the Eisenhowers set a new record for the number of Christmas trees used in decorating. In 1959, there were twenty-six trees! Lillian Rogers Parks said: "There was even one in the laundry room and another in the maids' sitting room. And David had his own private tree for his presents in the children's quarters on the third floor. That's because he had awakened one year at 3 A.M. and gotten the President and everyone up at that horrible hour with his squealing over the presents under the tree."

In 1962 the General Electric Company donated 4,000 ornaments and 5,000 lights for the 65-foot blue spruce given by Colorado and for the fifty-three smaller trees. That year, also, eight reindeer from Washington's National Zoological Park took up residence on the Ellipse for the duration of the pageant. A huge Yule log burned night and day for the comfort of participants.

The U.S. Army Chorus and Band kicked off the fifteen-day pageant with a seasonal concert at Constitution Hall on December

15. Traditional music was sung throughout the day on the Ellipse. Churches of all denominations, civic groups, labor and government organizations, and embassies all pitched in to make the pageant a success—a pattern that has been repeated every year.

Jacqueline Kennedy made a few innovations at the White House. Instead of the "Silver Tree" in the East Room, traditionally decorated with white electric candles and silver tinsel, Mrs. Kennedy erected a "Nutcracker" tree and placed it in the Blue Room. Sugarplum fairies, dancing flowers, flutes, and snowflakes replaced the traditional balls and tinsel.

For their last White House Christmas, the Lyndon Johnsons erected a gingerbread tree. It was a 20-foot white pine trimmed in nineteenth-century American style, featuring gingerbread cookies. It, too, graced the Blue Room.

Two years later, the White Mountain Apache Indians of Arizona donated a stately 75-foot Colorado blue spruce. It was the first tree ever given by an American Indian Tribal Council.

The arrival of the National Christmas Tree has taken on a ceremony of its own. The 1965 tree arrived on an 80-foot railroad flatcar and was moved from the old Baltimore and Ohio Railroad yards in Georgetown to the Ellipse. Pepco provided its largest crane to lift the tree from the flatcar onto a waiting truck. A five-foot-deep hole had been prepared for the tree, and it was supported by wires and cables. The trimming took several days. Later, Mrs. Gerald Ford found it exciting to wait for the arrival of the White House tree too. This she placed in the Blue Room.

Since President Lyndon Johnson was touring Asia and cheering U.S. troops in Vietnam in 1965, Vice-President Hubert Humphrey presided. In 1961, then Vice-President Johnson had subbed for President Kennedy, when JFK had flown to Palm Beach to be with his stricken father.

In 1967 a choral group from a foreign country made its first appearance. The Festival Singers of Toronto, Canada, sang "Now, O Zion, Gladly Rise" and the "Wassail Song." President Johnson brought his dog Yuki to the lighting ceremony, but the frisky animal could not sit still and had to be led off the stage by a presidential aide.

Mrs. Richard Nixon is responsible for several lovely customs. It was she who first established the candlelight tours of the White House at Christmastime. Thousands of visitors descend upon the President's House each year from 10 A.M. to 12 noon on Tuesdays

49

*Lynda Johnson Robb and her children
enjoy the 1968 "gingerbread tree"*

through Saturdays. It is widely agreed that the White House looks more beautiful at Christmas than at any other time. Mrs. Nixon felt that visitors would appreciate the decorations more if they could be viewed by the soft glow of candlelight, so the White House announced that visitors would be admitted for several additional hours on two evenings during the holiday season. This innovation has proved to be popular, and the Fords, Carters, and Reagans have continued it. The White House draws about 10,000 tourists during the Christmas season, which usually begins around December 7 or 8.

Patricia Nixon personally supervised the Christmas decorations during her first year as First Lady, in 1969. She made numerous changes. For the first time in twenty-five years, green wreaths and candles were placed in all sixteen windows facing Pennsylvania Avenue. Another first was the hanging of red, blue, and gold balls from the chandeliers in the halls, which reflected the light of candles that wore red-satin sleeves. These were old family traditions, Mrs. Nixon explained. The whole mansion seemed awash in poinsettias, holly, and greens. Red-velvet reindeer with silver antlers were placed on the marble mantels in the East Room.

The tree in the foyer was decorated with eight-inch velvet and satin Christmas balls embossed with the flowers of each of the fifty states.

There were some problems at the Pageant of Peace, however, For the first time since the ceremony had begun, almost fifty years before, the President was heckled by a chanting crowd of antiwar protesters. Mr. Nixon was forced to raise his voice during his remarks. When the President talked about the blessings of prosperity and his hopes for peace, the two hundred protesters began jeering loudly. About one-half hour before the President's arrival, U.S. Park Police arrested eight adults and one teenager on disorderly conduct charges.

Then the American Civil Liberties Union (ACLU) tried to remove the nativity scene from the Ellipse. The ACLU, representing three clergymen, an athiest, and a leader of the American Ethical Society, claimed that government sponsorship of a distinctively Christian symbol amounted to an unconstitutional establishment of religion. The pageant sponsors, who had an exclusive permit from the Interior Department for all events on the Ellipse, countered that the nativity scene was a "reminder of our spiritual heritage."

The ACLU sought to block construction of the crèche in 1969 until the constitutional issues could be resolved. The U.S. Court of Appeals ruled on December 12, 1969, that the crèche be allowed that year. The case dragged on for almost four years. Finally on September 26, 1973, the Court of Appeals ruled in favor of the plaintiffs and against the crèche. The Department of the Interior and the National Park Service, both government agencies, were responsible for the program, so the court held that such sponsorship was tantamount to government support for religion.

The three-judge panel ruled that the nativity scene had to be dropped from the pageant or the government had to end its role in the display in order to limit "excessive entanglement" between government and religion. So, the crèche vanished in 1973.

In 1970, the tree was trouble-dogged. The train bringing it to Washington was involved in not one but two derailments. It finally limped into town on November 25. Then, on December 6, high winds and freezing rain tore into the national capital and felled many trees. One of its victims was the 78-foot spruce from South Dakota. It was blown flat on its side. A number of persons who had gone to the Ellipse to watch the trimming had to flee quickly as the tree swayed and then tumbled to the ground.

The tree finally made it to the ceremonies. President Richard Nixon also had a little help at the annual lighting ceremony. He walked into the throng of 10,000 and selected a tiny five-year-old boy, André Proctar, to help him push the button. A driving rain quickly reduced the crowd. As the rain-drenched crowd began to file out, the President concluded by saying, "If you're not all completely doused, before we leave, let's sing 'Joy to the World!'" The few hardy souls remaining sang lustily.

In 1974, the Colonial Williamsburg Foundation offered to decorate the Blue Room tree with thousands of antique hand-carved wooden ornaments. Betty Ford said she "breathed a great sigh of relief." (In 1970 and 1971 Saks Fifth Avenue had trimmed the tree.)

International events have a way of spoiling the simple joys of

The main tree for the Nixons' 1970 Christmas

Christmas. In 1979 and again in 1980, President Jimmy Carter left the giant Ellipse tree in darkness, except for the star on top, as a symbol of America's anger and disgust at the Iranian seizure of American citizens and the holding of them as hostages. There were lights on the fifty smaller trees surrounding the National Christmas Tree, however. In 1979 Mr. Carter lighted a menorah in Lafayette Park, given by the Jewish Community. The menorah symbolizes Hanukkah, an eight-day celebration generally taking place near Christmas.

Betty Ford said that the White House became a "fabulous fairyland" at Christmas. Many people would agree.

In 1981, the main tree in the Blue Room was 19½ feet high and was decorated by handmade ornaments contributed by the Museum of American Folk Art in New York. It was topped by Gabriel the Archangel. There were two trees with real candles (unlighted) in the North Entrance Hall and six trees with white lights in the East Room. Nancy Reagan spent part of two days decorating the Blue Room tree. The Reagans also decorated a tree for their private quarters on the second floor. Mrs. Reagan said the President would help because "he's pretty good at it."

The White House is always awash with poinsettias, holly, and evergreens. Dorothy Temple, the White House florist, and thirty volunteers decorated the old house in 1981. One of the White House chefs, Hans Raffert, made the traditional gingerbread house and added a walkway made out of jelly beans. The dollhouse, created by interior designer Aline Koplin Gray of Philadelphia, and the exquisite Italian baroque crèche, given by Mrs. Charles W. Engelhard, Jr., to Lady Bird Johnson in 1967, both graced the Blue Room.

Ronald Reagan turned on the lights on the giant Colorado spruce on the Ellipse from the White House on December 17. The threat of an assassination from a Libyan hit squad made it impossible for the President to appear in person. The National Christmas Tree had 10,000 lights, blue being the dominant color. An unusual decoration consisted of thirteen big triangle-shaped stars, each representing one of the original colonies.

Mr. Reagan delivered a special Christmas message to the American people on December 23 from the Oval Office, which was decorated with evergreens, red candles, and poinsettias.

54

5
Parties

It would be a rare Christmas without a party of some sort. Parties at the White House during the Christmas season began in the early days of the presidency, though without some of the gusto of today's festivities.

The custom throughout the nineteenth century and until the Coolidge Administration was for the President to hold a "levee" on New Year's Day. This was a stiff, formal gathering in which the President greeted guests at the door, shook their hands and engaged in a bit of conversation. In the informal early days of the Republic, anyone who wished would be admitted to the White House. A similar levee was held on July 4.

In her biography of Abigail Adams, Janet Whitney describes the first levee ever held at the White House in Washington:

"In January 1801 the first New Year reception was held in the President's House. Many candles and roaring fires did their best to make a festive air. The President and his wife received their guests in the beautiful oval room, with their red furniture from Auteuil, and gave Washington its first sensation of being a society. Foreign ministers wore their orders, gentlemen their snowy powder, their bags and swords. Ladies decorated the scene with their elaborate dresses. Washington, D.C., took a definite step from looking like a trading post to looking like the capital of a great nation."

The first record we have of a grand Christmas party is that of 1811, when vivacious Dolly Madison was First Lady. (A children's party when John Adams was President is described in Ch. 3, "The Pitter-Patter of Little Feet.") The coveted invitations to guests read simply, "President Madison and I would be greatly honored to have you dine with us on Christmas evening."

On the appointed night, Dolly Madison sat regally at the head of a long table in the State Dining Room. The guests were distinguished. They included Henry Clay, John Randolph, and Secretary of State James Monroe. (Where was the Vice-President? He was nowhere to be seen. As several wags expressed it, whoever was elected Vice-President was generally never heard from again.) Dolly's sisters Anna and Lucy were radiantly present. Washington Irving, then the literary rage, called the three sisters "the Merry Wives of Windsor." Several notable beauties of the day added to the pleasure of the gentlemen.

The gentlemen wore light-blue or green frock coats, garnished with gilt or pearl buttons, and tall shirt collars reaching to their ears. James Monroe, though, insisted on wearing a powdered wig, knee breeches, black silk stockings, and buckled pumps.

President Madison, however, wore his usual black "small clothes," black stockings, and a wig. Washington Irving was singularly unimpressed by Madison's sartorial indifference. "Poor Jemmy Madison—he is but a withered little applejohn," Irving wrote after a White House visit. (Madison's nickname was Jemmy, and at five feet six inches he was our shortest President.) Another writer called Madison "sallow, solemn and studious."

Dolly, on the other hand, was the life of the party. A contemporary account of the 1811 affair described her:

"Mr. Madison is content to occupy the background at any sort of entertainment in the White House. His wife is the conspicuous figure dominating the brilliant scene on this Christmas evening, as always when festivities are in progress. She is a magnificent looking woman, forty-three years old (on this point there is a little dispute) tall, stately, buxom and rosy. Anxious to delay the flight of time as manifested in her own charming person, she wears much rouge—enough indeed to be perceptible in a very bright light. People say of her that she insists on staying the same age for many years together."

Dolly wore a vivid purple velvet dress, pearls, and many bracelets. She had redecorated the State Dining Room with mirrors and a solid silver candelabra that held over a hundred candles. There were banks of flowers.

Dolly had haggled with furniture dealers to get the most for her money. Congress had provided only $11,000 to refurbish the executive mansion. (Actually, the mansion was not white at that time. It was built of Virginia sandstone and appeared brown in color. It was also called the President's Palace rather than executive mansion or White House.) Dolly's crowning achievement was yellow satin over the fireplace.

Entertaining in 1811 was quite inexpensive. Turkeys cost 75 cents apiece, ducks 50 cents, and a whole suckling pig only $3.00. Waiters, who were generally slaves rented by their masters for a day, were paid 35 cents for an evening party.

E. Pendleton Hogan described the dinner.

"After the Virginia country manner all the food was put on the table at once. Turkeys, chickens, canvas-back ducks, and roasted wild game. Vegetables, fruit and several kinds of pudding. For every guest there was a waiter, extra ones having been hired for the occasion.

"Dinner lasted for one hour, and then Colonel Monroe offered the customary toast, drunk standing, to the ladies. This was the signal for the ladies to withdraw; the ladies withdrew. Then with the Yuletide custom of Colonial days a great punchbowl was brought into the dining room and the gentlemen began their really serious drinking. A few glasses made even Mr. Madison relax and become anecdotal, and it is said that he knew some good stories. Finally, upon Mr. Madison's suggestion, the gentlemen rejoined the ladies in the Oval Room, which is now the Blue Room."

After dinner Dolly Madison initiated a number of popular games. Then came singing and dancing. But revelers retired early in those days. By ten o'clock the guests began to depart. Their carriages arrived at the South Entrance, where the regally attired guests had to fight their way through a mudhole before entering their carriages. All in all, it was a splendid evening.

An amusing incident transpired on Christmas Eve in 1815. Mrs. Madison brought her pet macaw into the dining room to amuse the children and guests at her annual Christmas party. But the bird ran after a young guest named Mary and attached itself to the child's feet. The terrified girl screamed and jumped onto a chair, clutching the First Lady. Mrs. Madison thought it was all "quite a frolic."

Guns fired all night—a custom associated with Southern Christmases in those days. The Madisons were happy that Christmas, because the War of 1812 had ended and because Dolly's troublesome son Payne was home. Dolly created her special cinnamon-sprinkled eggnog and tried to re-create a Virginia plantation Christmas, complete with candlelight, holly, and running cedar.

A lively dance was held in the East Room in late December, 1828, to celebrate the departure of John Quincy and Louisa Adams from the White House. Adams had been defeated for re-election a month earlier. The U.S. Marine Band played the latest tunes. The ladies wore elegant gowns and the officers were resplendent in their dress uniforms. The President looked happy. He greeted guests jovially and danced the Virginia Reel.

In 1844, President John Tyler's spirited second wife, Julia, had decorated the White House with wreaths of evergreen. Even the portrait of George Washington, which gazed down on the festive scene, was clad in holiday greenery. The food was again reminiscent of Virginia plantation fare, varied and bountiful. The First Lady was obviously enjoying the season. She reported to her diary, "We commenced the day with eggnog and concluded with apple toddy." Parties abounded at "Julia's court."

Even the sober President and Mrs. James K. Polk gave a reception on Christmas Eve 1847. The only account of that evening came from a Washington correspondent who was present. His report concentrated on the guest list and the clothing styles rather than on the spirit of Christmas. His rather tongue-in-cheek commentary included these observations:

"Last evening I had an opportunity of seeing the members of the royal family, together with some choice specimens of the Democracy in the 'circle room' of the White House. It was reception night and the latch-string in the shape of a handsome negro was 'outside the door.' On entering I found a comfortable room full, with a little man, whom I would have taken in any other place for a Methodist parson, standing before the fire, bowing and shaking hands in the most precise and indiscriminate manner. He is affable and ordinary enough in conversation to prevent one from feeling that he is in direct communication with the concentrated Majesty of the whole United States and Territories. Mr. Polk is not a man to inspire awe.

"The better half of the President was seated on the sofa, engaged with some half a dozen ladies in lively conversation."

Among the guests were politicians, bankers, financiers, and military officers. Present also were "two pretty deaf and dumb girls who talked with their fingers and scores of other attractive women who only talked with their eyes," according to the

President and Mrs. Grant held a "brilliant"
Christmas dinner in honor of the King of
Hawaii, December 23, 1874

report of this observant journalist.

One of the strangest Christmas "parties" took place in 1860, when the lonely bachelor, President James Buchanan, invited a delegation of Pawnee Indians to a gathering at the White House during the holidays. The Indians were somewhat ill at ease with their Great White Father.

Two years later, the city of Washington was full of wounded soldiers in numerous hospitals. The women of the city had arranged parties to be held at each hospital. President and Mrs. Lincoln and some cabinet members visited the hospital on Judiciary Square in the afternoon of Christmas Day. They were pleased with the thoughtfulness and generosity shown to the recuperating soldiers.

On December 23, 1874, President and Mrs. Grant held a Christmas dinner in honor of the King of Hawaii. The White House was brilliantly illuminated. The East Room was described as "brilliant beyond all precedent" and "magnificent." In the Green Room was a new life-size picture of General Grant on horseback. It had been painted in New Orleans and presented to the President for Christmas. New crystal chandeliers gave an added beauty to the room and picture.

Teddy Roosevelt's last Christmas in the White House, in 1908, was the scene of a special party. His seventeen-year-old daughter Ethel's debut on December 28 was called by the press "the grandest Christmas Party since the Civil War."

One account says, "The entire suite of state apartments was thrown open, and the hundreds of guests made their way up the grand stairway into the lobby, where the portraits of Presidents gazed across banks of Christmas greens and rows of huge vases holding whole trees of holly."

Because of the presence of young adults in the presidential families, Christmas parties for young people enlivened the Administrations of Coolidge, Hoover, FDR, Truman, Johnson, and Ford. The Roosevelt children were always bringing home friends for the holidays. And where there were friends, there were parties.

President and Mrs. Theodore Roosevelt restored
the "old-time gaiety" to society in Washington

The first Christmas party of the Herbert Hoovers was nearly a disaster, for a fire nearly burned down the White House. Here is how it happened.

The Christmas of 1929 was frigid in more ways than one. The stock market crash, heralding the Great Depression, was fresh in everyone's mind, as was the certainty of bad times. The weather was frosty. Snow lay on the ground, and ice frosted the window-panes.

At the White House, though, a festive spirit prevailed. President and Mrs. Herbert Hoover were welcoming the children of the President's staff at a party. Most were young, but a few were in their late teens and early twenties. They congregated around the President's son Allen, home from Harvard for the holidays. A scarlet-coated contingent of the U.S. Marine Band played carols in the East Room. Dinner, refreshments, games, and presents were on the evening agenda.

In the West Wing of the White House, a skeleton staff preserved security. A Secret Service operative, a policeman, and a switchboard operator were the only ones manning the Christmas Eve shift. The President's Oval Office, the press room, and the clerical offices were all quiet. Above the main floor was an attic crammed with papers of every sort.

Shortly after 8 P.M. the switchboard operator, M. M. Rice, saw wisps of smoke near his station. He immediately phoned the Secret Service, the White House police office, and chief usher Irwin (Ike) Hoover, the legendary majordomo to nine Presidents.

A few moments later an office messenger, Charlie Williamson, smelled smoke fumes. He ran directly into Secret Service agent Russell Wood and policeman Richard Trice. The three men knew something was wrong. Tracing the now-thickening smoke, Wood and Trice mounted a stairway to the attic. There they encountered a wall of flames. One of them ran to turn in an alarm. The others sought a fire extinguisher.

But nothing happened when the main lighting switch was pulled. Fire had burned the wires away. It was inside the partitions. The whole place was on fire. Fortunately the White House fire alarm box worked. A team of engines was soon tearing through deserted Washington streets, heading for the big house at 1600 Pennsylvania Avenue.

Meanwhile, back at the State Dining Room, chief usher Hoover notified Larry Richey, the President's personal secretary,

*The Franklin Roosevelts welcomed their son home
for Christmas with gay holiday decorations*

and the President himself. They all rushed to the scene, concerned about the number of valuable public and personal documents that were imperiled.

The President hastily donned a heavy blue overcoat and gray fedora over his dinner jacket and raced to the South Lawn to see the flames. He hurried to save some papers from his office, but was hustled away by worried Secret Service agents. Mr. Hoover then went to the roof of the adjacent conservatory, the long low wing known as the West Terrace, which connects the White House and the Executive Offices. There he lighted a cigar and viewed the proceedings.

The fire threatened to get out of control. Sixteen engines had come through the White House gates. Several of Mr. Hoover's secretaries and his son Allen braved the flames to save some personal files and documents and the chairs that were used for cabinet meetings. At times it appeared as if the flames were subdued, but there were occasional bursts of blaze through the roof, causing the firemen considerable difficulty. Four firemen were overcome by the staggering heat. By 9:24 P.M. five alarms had been sounded.

Enormous amounts of water had to be used to douse the stubborn flames. So, what the flames did not destroy, water did. Fortunately many valuable documents had been removed during a remodeling a few months before.

In the basement, working by kerosene lantern, switchboard operator Rice stayed by his post until, knee deep in icy water, he was ordered to leave. Six firemen were flattened when the ceiling in the President's office crashed down on them. Two were hurt by the falling crystal chandelier, but the remaining four were miraculously unhurt. Outside, the streets and walls and firemen were covered by a sheet of ice.

News of the fire spread rapidly and crowds soon gathered. Secretary of War Patrick Hurley ordered 150 soldiers from Fort McNair (then called the Washington Barracks) to surround the White House and hold back the crowds. Across the Potomac River at Fort Myer, a troop of the 3d Cavalry was standing by in case it was needed. One hundred men of the Metropolitan Police supplemented the Army troops.

President Hoover nervously paced back and forth, puffing on his cigar. He was cheered by the courageous bravado of Honorary Deputy Chief Henry C. Stein, who charged into the President's office to save the President's personal silk flag. Dressed in boots, waterproof coat, and white helmet, Stein emerged with the flag intact, and great cheers went up from the crowd.

It was soon evident that the President's office was ruined. The officer in charge of D.C. public buildings was then Lieutenant Colonel U. S. Grant III, the grandson of President Grant. Leaving his Christmas Eve dinner, Grant spent most of the night trying to locate a new office for the Chief Executive. Eventually Mr. Hoover used the office of the former Chief of Staff, General John J. Pershing.

The executive offices were unusable and would have to be rebuilt. The President's staff were housed temporarily in the State, War, and Navy Department Buildings across West Executive Avenue.

Mrs. Hoover kept the Christmas Eve party going at full swing. Many of the guests did not even know there was a fire. The President finally wound down and went to bed around midnight.

At 7:27 on Christmas morning, the White House fire was officially declared out, almost twelve hours after it started. The cause of the fire was discovered to be an overheated flue in the open fireplace of a secretary's office. Fifteen firemen had been injured, but the President's House was saved.

At Christmas in 1934, President and Mrs. Roosevelt welcomed their sons, Franklin, Jr., and John, home from school for the holidays, with a dinner dance. The mansion was decked in holiday dress. Four Christmas trees, brilliantly lighted and shining under the white portico facing Pennsylvania Avenue, greeted the three hundred guests as they arrived.

In the East Room, where the dance was held, a Christmas tree stood in the recessed windows, and Christmas greens and holly, interspersed with red poinsettias, banked the four mantels.

Eleanor Roosevelt enjoyed giving dinner dances for the "young set." She liked to invite engaged and young married couples. Generally, Meyer Davis' orchestra would play, and a delightful "supper" was served.

The staff was highly amused by Mrs. Roosevelt's custom of serving raw onions with the scrambled eggs and sausages. "She gets all those romantic young couples and then tries to kill the romance," commented a White House maid.

But she was kind and generous. She waited on the others and ate her plate on the backstairs steps after everyone had been served. She also enjoyed the Virginia Reel with her brother.

Mamie Eisenhower gave a tea party for newspaperwomen, beginning in 1957. Male reporters were excluded! Mamie loved to supervise the decorations of the White House in time for the party. Wrote Bess Furman of the 1957 party, "There were great bouquets of red poinsettias combined with holly in the East Room, hall and foyer; pink poinsettias in the Green Room; frosty white branches in the Blue Room; and white poinsettias in the Red Room where Mrs. Eisenhower received her guests."

Standing in the receiving line with Mrs. Eisenhower were Alice Roosevelt Longworth, Perle Mesta, and Mrs. Merriweather Post.

The Kennedys and the Johnsons expanded the First Family's party-giving. The diplomatic corps had a party of their own. Then the children of the diplomats were invited to a special party.

By 1979, there was a full array of parties. The Carters' Christmas season began on December 5, when one thousand people, mostly members of Congress and their spouses, came to a ball. Peter Duchin and his orchestra played in the East Room. Tables were laden with smoked trout and salmon, crab claws, ham, roast beef, marinated artichokes and mushrooms, cheese ring, fruitcake, a chocolate Yule log, eggnog, champagne and other wines, and a Christmas punch.

On the very next night, the Carters hosted five hundred members of the Washington press corps. Then there were parties for the White House staff, the Secret Service, and the children of diplomats. In 1980, the Carters gave a dinner for the Cabinet and the White House senior staff, in addition to the other parties.

In 1981, Nancy Reagan invited the press for a sneak preview of the White House decorations a day before the general public was admitted. She served coffee and pastries.

All of this party-giving rather bewildered Mrs. Betty Ford. In her autobiography, *The Times of My Life,* she wrote: "The Christmas parties started, and I didn't think they'd ever stop. There was a party at the Hospital for Sick Children, and I went and helped Santa Claus distribute gifts. There was a White House party for the children of the diplomatic corps, and after that, a practically identical party for the children of the cooks, maids, and anybody else who worked in the White House. There were parties for kids, and parties for grownups. We gave a Christmas party for the members of the White House press. . . .

"We gave an honest-to-goodness ball that season too: the first

Annual Christmas Ball in years for the Cabinet and members of Congress. It had occurred to me that the White House looked so beautiful during the holidays that it would be an ideal time to entertain the Congress with a great black-tie gathering. And it was in the Blue Room, Jerry pointed to the magnificent tree that stretched clear to the ceiling and told the thousand guests—from the Hill, the Cabinet, the senior White House staff—that he and the Christmas tree, also from Michigan, had a lot in common. 'A few months ago, neither one of us expected to be in the White House.'"

6
Gifts

Christmas would hardly be Christmas without the exchange of gifts. Records of the early Presidents are quite sketchy as far as Christmas gifts are concerned. We do know that Andrew Jackson loved to lavish saddles, hobbyhorses, and wax dolls on his grand-nieces and grandnephews. Abraham Lincoln loved to do his own Christmas shopping, as did William Howard Taft and Woodrow Wilson.

Every Christmas Eve while he was President, Lincoln would walk slowly along New York Avenue until he reached the vicinity of Twelfth Street. There he would enter a quaint little toy shop presided over by a Crimean War veteran. Toy soldiers were the object of his quest, for Tad, his beloved little boy, adored them and always could use "just a few more" for their sham battles.

Passersby could see the tall, gaunt President, his shawl closely drawn about him, listening to the old Crimean warrior demon-strating the great battles of that campaign with toy soldiers.

On Christmas Eve in 1909, President Taft left the White House on foot to shop on Pennsylvania Avenue and F Street, returning long after dark, laden down with bundles. The Presi-dent could be heard chuckling, because his aide, Captain Archie Butt, was also carrying an enormous number of gifts.

Wilson usually tried to do his shopping early. One year he was seen in the shops on December 1. In 1916, after his reelection, Wilson and his wife, Edith, went shopping together. An amusing incident is told by Mrs. Wilson: "My husband and I squeezed in one little Christmas shopping tour together. At Becker's leather store a clerk was so shy that he could hardly articulate. Showing the President a bag with a removable watch he said: 'You could take it out and make a wist wrotch out of it.' He tried the sentence again, with the same result, and was about to retire in confusion when my husband said: 'A capital idea. I have always wanted a wrist watch and never have had one. I think I'll take the bag to get the watch.' The poor man beamed at him."

In 1922, Warren Harding's purchase of books for friends in a Washington bookstore moved the venerable *New York Times* to praise the President editorially. The President did not want to be seen. He went shopping late, strode briskly, and wore a black overcoat and a brown hat pulled low over his forehead!

Rutherford B. Hayes loved to buy presents for his children. In his meticulously kept diary of his presidency, Hayes recorded these events:

December 25, 1877—"Christmas, the presents to the children made them and their parents equally happy."

December 25, 1878—"A happy day for Fanny and Scott. More presents than ever before. But a long day!"

December 25, 1879—"This Christmas day is given up to the little folks, Fanny and Scott."

Hayes appears to have inaugurated the custom of giving gifts to the presidential household, servants and staff. In 1880 he gave each one a $5.00 gold piece. (Hayes, incidentally, is one of three Presidents who kept a diary of his days in the White House. John Quincy Adams and James K. Polk were the others.)

Mrs. Hayes enjoyed her shopping excursions. The Washington *National Republican* sent a reporter to cover her shopping tour of Pennsylvania Avenue on Christmas Eve, 1880. He reported: "From the extended shopping tour made by Mrs. Hayes on the Avenue yesterday, it can be safely asserted that the little folks at the White House will find that Kris Kringle did not carry a light load when he climbed down the chimney and tackled the stockings in that historic mansion."

Colonel William H. Crook, a bodyguard to President Lincoln and a White House staff member for five Presidents, was delighted by the Hayeses' gift-giving ceremony. He wrote: "At Christmastime Mrs. Hayes had a present for every one of the household, secretaries, clerks, doorkeepers. Sometimes she bought the presents herself, in which case she would be at work for weeks beforehand. Sometimes, when she was rushed, she commissioned Webb Hayes and me to buy them. At those times there would be a card for each one, to give the more personal touch. At about noon on Christmas Day everyone was called into the library.

*Christmas shopping in 1882, from a drawing
in* Frank Leslie's Weekly

There, in a heap in the middle of the floor, were the presents.
Beside them waited President and Mrs. Hayes, and little Miss
Fanny and Scott waited 'first on one foot and then on t'other' for
the festivities to begin. The President or his wife read out the
names and picked out the presents, and the two children danced
about distributing them. I remember my gift the first year was a
fine plated silver water pitcher, which I am still using. It was a real
Christmas that came to the White House in those days, and Mrs.
Hayes's smile was better than eggnog."

William McKinley gave each member of the staff a photograph or a book. Theodore Roosevelt gave each clerk a $5.00 gold

piece and each policeman and messenger a turkey. William Howard Taft, however, chose to ignore this custom, to the surprise and dismay of the staff. Ira R. T. Smith, a White House employee, remembered: "It had been customary for the President to give each White House employee a Christmas gift. When this custom was brought to Mr. Taft's attention at the proper time, he remarked: 'I don't see why I should have to give them anything.' And he didn't."

Woodrow Wilson, however, gave turkeys to all married White House employees. The Hardings returned to the custom of giving a $5.00 gold piece to every staff person.

Calvin Coolidge was no lavish gift giver. According to Drew Pearson and Robert S. Allen, White House staffers insisted that Coolidge had given "pass-me-ons," or hand-me-downs, to his staff. Coolidge also had a puckish sense of humor. Washington hostess and popular novelist Frances Parkinson Keyes, in her *Capital Kaleidoscope,* recorded that Coolidge gave her a box of cactus candy for Christmas one year. It came in a brilliantly decorated yellow satin box. Coolidge told her: "It's a good kind of candy for writers. You ought to eat a lot of it." Mrs. Keyes never did figure out what he meant by that gift.

Longtime White House usher Alonzo Fields told in his memoir how the Hoovers celebrated Christmas with the staff. "Christmas with the Hoovers had been a time of cordial but reserved master-to-servantlike greetings. President and Mrs. Hoover would come into the East Room and say 'Merry Christmas' to all the household staff gathered around the big tree in that room. Gifts would be passed out—an autographed picture and an envelope with a crisp new $5 bill for servants of the lower bracket, and larger amounts for those of the higher brackets. Then President and Mrs. Hoover would bow and leave and there would be no handshaking."

The irrepressible Franklin Roosevelts started the practice of personally greeting all of the staff, including their families and children. FDR shook the hands of everyone, while Eleanor passed out presents in the East Room. Hundreds came for these annual bashes, usually held on the Sunday afternoon nearest to Christmas Day. In 1933, FDR gave autographed copies of his book *Looking Forward* to the clerical and the administrative staff. In 1934 he repeated this with autographed copies of his *On Our Way.* After that, he passed out crisp new dollar bills.

70

*Eleanor Roosevelt enjoyed choosing personally
gifts for everyone on the White House staff*

Eleanor Roosevelt loved Christmas shopping so much that she
did it all year long, beginning in January. She was eclectic in her
choices. One year she purchased pottery from a wayside stand in
New England, baskets from a New York school for the blind,
neckties from an orphanage in her home county, Dutchess
County, New York, pewter from a local New York shop, furniture
from a mountaineer handicraft shop in Reidsville, West Virginia,
and embroidered rugs from Berea College in Kentucky. She knew
and loved her staff well, from footmen to cooks to maids to policemen. She selected personalized gifts for everyone, and kept lists

71

from year to year to minimize the chance of repeating a particular present. The Roosevelt children, however, used to complain that their mother only picked "sensible" gifts for them.

It is little wonder that columnist Beatrice Fairfax wrote in 1934, "The members of the White House family are the greatest Christmas fans in the U.S." To which Mrs. Roosevelt responded: "Christmas is the way we'd like to feel toward everyone, every day in the year—the good will, the fellowship, the hope for better things—but these sincere sentiments are crowded out by the pressure of everyday demands. If only we had time, we'd like every day to have this spirit of Christmas."

Lillian Rogers Parks could hardly believe the care that Mrs. Roosevelt took in selecting gifts for the staff. She wrote: "As far as Mrs. Roosevelt was concerned, one of my biggest jobs was to make large red stockings for all the grandchildren and some adults, to be hung on Christmas Eve. Christmas was the real fun time for the First Lady, the time of year when she seemed to be most thrilled and happy.

"Christmas started in October for Eleanor Roosevelt. There was a room on the third floor that we called the toy room, in which she would stack all of her presents. She shopped with loving care for everyone. There were over a hundred policemen, and one year it would be neckties for them, and the next year it might be pocketknives or handkerchiefs. Then she would shop for the chauffeurs, the soldiers who attended the riding horses at Fort Myer, the carpenters, plumbers, electricians, painters, florists, groundsmen, cooks, butlers, maids, housemen, valets, doormen, and the rest. To top it off, she would buy gifts for the children under twelve of all the White House backstairs family."

The Eisenhowers also loved to share their holiday with the White House staff. Mamie Eisenhower began the custom of serving delectable food when she and the President greeted their staff and passed out presents. This party was generally held on Christmas Eve at 11 A.M.

Lillian Rogers Parks wrote that "Mrs. Eisenhower was the most generous and thoughtful gift giver in my memory. Her last gift to me was a beautiful leather book cover with my name engraved on it in gold."

Like his friend Winston Churchill, Dwight Eisenhower was a weekend painter. Thus, for six of his eight years as President, Mr. Eisenhower presented his staff with color prints of his own paintings. In 1953, Ike painted Abraham Lincoln, from a photograph taken in 1863. Ike had begun "idly sketching" the photograph in July and finished it a few days later. In 1954 he painted a copy of a Gilbert Stuart painting of George Washington. In 1955 his landscape of a favorite fishing stream, St. Louis Creek, was given to employees. In 1958 his painting *Deserted Barn* was the gift. A painting of Mt. Eisenhower in the Canadian Rockies for 1959 was followed the next year by his view of a Bavarian church scene.

On two occasions the staff received photographs. The 1956 one presented the First Lady in her inaugural gown, and in 1957 the photograph depicted the Green Room. The staff grew from

President and Mrs. Kennedy make their entrance
. to the annual staff Christmas party

600 to 1100 during the Eisenhower days. The executive office staff, the Secret Service, the White House police, military units assigned to the White House, and the domestic staff were always included.

The Kennedys gave their 1962 staff prints of a watercolor of the Red Room. Each was mounted in a matching red folder bearing the presidential seal. The original painting, by Edward Lehman of Quakertown, Pennsylvania, was placed in the private quarters of the First Family. That year JFK was so eager to greet his guests that he almost knocked some of the glittering ornaments off the tree in the Blue Room.

One Christmas President and Mrs. Nixon presented their staff with color prints of Gilbert Stuart's famous 1796 painting of George Washington.

Some of our Presidents received numerous gifts from the folks back home. While this is no longer the custom, it was generally thought appropriate to send gifts to the White House. In 1913, Woodrow Wilson received an unusual gift from Levi N. Ludlum of Wichita, Kansas. He sent Andrew Jackson's walking stick. Ludlum had received the cane from a friend in Tennessee, who told him to give it to a Democratic President.

In 1926, Yule gifts flooded the White House. The turkeys and hams given to the Coolidges were distributed to local hospitals and orphanages. President Coolidge received a diverse array of presents from well-wishers. Included were a dozen canes, boxes of cigars and cigar holders, handkerchiefs, stockings, ties, and gloves. The West Room of the White House was piled high with presents.

In 1929, Mrs. Hoover selected a number of travel and mystery books for her husband. She visited area bookstores and selected titles personally, until the press of official business made her delegate the task to secretaries. But she carefully prepared the list of desired titles. Hoover, like Wilson before him and FDR after him, enjoyed mystery and suspense novels. A popular mystery writer of that day, Carolyn Wells, dedicated one of her Fleming Stone novels to Mr. Hoover. Wilson's favorite mystery writer was J. S. Fletcher, while FDR cherished the Lord Peter Wimsey novels of Dorothy L. Sayers.

The Eisenhowers received some unusual gifts. In 1954 a 100-pound cake shaped like a Christmas tree and standing 5½ feet tall was sent to the First Family by the Young Men's Republican Club of Niagara Falls, New York. The cook, Mrs. Alberta Dust, said she had used thirty pounds of butter in the cake. Ike sent it to Walter

74

Reed Army Hospital. The following year the same group sent an 800-pound fruitcake shaped like a red-brick fireplace. Ike sent it to the Washington Home for the Aged. In 1957 a group of admirers in St. Mary's County, Maryland, sent the President a 42-pound turkey and two gallons of oysters.

In 1959, Premier Nikita Khrushchev sent the President a beautiful collection of Russian toys and dolls. Included were Christmas tree ornaments and lights and forty-one trees and shrubs for the President's Gettysburg farm. A special Soviet plane brought the gifts from the Soviet leader, who had visited the United States a few weeks before.

Presidential gift-opening habits were sometimes unique. FDR refused to be hurried in opening his gifts. It often took him days to complete the ceremony. Once he spied a book that delighted him. He insisted on reading the whole thing before opening any additional presents several days later.

Harry Truman, on the other hand, loved to rip open all his presents as soon as they were deposited on his lap. And Lyndon Johnson insisted that his wife and daughters open all their presents at once and try on the clothing items he had selected.

7

Feasting

Sumptuous repasts have long been an integral part of Christmas. The basic holiday menu has not varied too much through the years. Jefferson served hot spiced brandy toddy. Washington and Madison served eggnog. Teddy Roosevelt loved champagne with his chicken sandwiches. FDR was also partial to champagne. Early White House cooks did their own marketing.

Wartime Christmases in the White House have been austere, both because of scarcities and because of the mood of the times. During the Civil War and the world wars, particularly, feasting was modest.

Henrietta Nesbitt, the housekeeper and cook whom the Roosevelts brought from Hyde Park to the White House, was a wizard at making fruitcake and plum pudding. These were FDR's favorite desserts, and Mrs. Nesbitt made them for him on his birthday and at Christmas. Mrs. Nesbitt recorded that the White House was "running over with rich foods and rich smells each Christmas season." She said, "December found me up to my ears in fruitcake." This is her recipe:

"Six pounds of cut dates. Six pounds of raisins. One and a half pounds of almonds, blanched and sliced lengthwise. Two and a fourth pounds of citron in long slivers. Three cups of orange peel also slivered.

In the early days, members of the White
House kitchen staff did their own marketing.
Cooks choose game and poultry in Lincoln's day

PACKER & KNAPP

"I take my time with the fruit fixing, and enjoy it. Then I pour a pint of brandy or rum over the mixed fruit and let it stand all night or longer. The batter I mix like a pound cake:

"One and a half pounds brown sugar. One and a half pounds butter. One and a half pounds flour. Eighteen eggs.

"To this mixture I add one and a half cups of honey, two grated lemon rinds, one and a half teaspoons each of mace, nutmeg, and salt, a fourth teaspoon of cloves, and three teaspoons of cinnamon.

"Then I mix in the fruit, and bake it in lined pans at a low oven temperature with a pan of water in the oven to keep the cake moist."

The Christmas of 1944 was a difficult one. Rationing and scarcity threatened to make the President's Christmas dinner a lean one. Mrs. Nesbitt sadly related that "fruitcakes were out that year. Materials were too hard to get, of too poor quality, and too high when you found them." But she insisted on making the plum pudding, for it pleased the President so much. She wrote: "But I made my mind up there would be a plum pudding on the Christmas table! That was the supreme moment of the Roosevelt year, when the pudding came in on its silver tray, set in holly, with the blue flame of the brandy lighting up the circle of old and young faces. No matter what President Roosevelt's worries were, he looked his happiest then. So I made the plum pudding." This is her recipe:

"One and a half pounds each of grated bread crumbs (use bread a day or two old), seeded raisins, currants, brown and white sugar (half and half). One pound kidney suet chopped fine. One half pound each mixed orange and lemon peel and cut walnuts. One teaspoon each nutmeg, mace, cinnamon, one fourth teaspoon cloves, and twelve eggs.

"I beat my sugar and eggs to a cream, mix in the suet and bread crumbs, then blend in everything; moisten with sherry, grape juice, or brandy, and steam in molds for three hours."

George Washington loved eggnog in the old Virginia style. This is his recipe:

"1 quart milk, 1 quart cream, 1 dozen eggs, 1 dozen tablespoons sugar, 1 pint brandy, ½ pint rye whiskey, ¼ pint Jamaica or New England rum, ¼ pint sherry.

"Mix liquor first. Separate yolks and whites of eggs. Add sugar to beaten yolks. Mix well. Add liquor mixture, drop by drop at first,

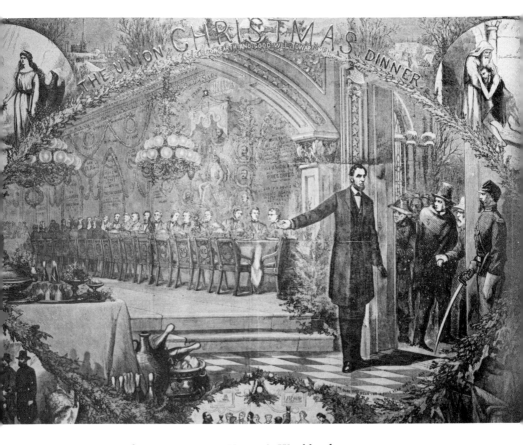

A Civil War cartoon in Harper's Weekly *shows mock banquet of the States, with President Lincoln inviting the southern states in to fill their empty chairs. Typical holiday foods and decorations are depicted*

slowly beating. Beat whites of eggs until stiff and fold slowly into mixture. Let set in cool place several days."

Though it may be impractical to make in today's kitchens without reducing the portions considerably, here is Martha Washington's recipe for a "great cake."

"Take 40 eggs & divide the whites from the youlks & beat them to a froth start work 4 pounds of butter to a cream & put the

79

whites of eggs to it a spoon full at a time till it is well work'd then put 4 pounds of sugar finely powdered to it in the same manner then put in the Youlks of eggs & 5 pounds of flower & 5 pounds of fruit. 2 hours will bake it add to it half an ounce of mace 1 nutmeg half a pint of wine & some french brandy." This recipe was supplied by the Mount Vernon Ladies' Association.

Christmas Day found the Carter family back home in Plains, Georgia. Early in the morning the entire Carter clan set out for Miss Lillian's house, where the President's mother laid on a Southern holiday breakfast of country ham, eggs, grits with cheese, homemade preserves, and coffee. Then the family moved on to Miss Allie's house. Miss Allie is Rosalynn Carter's mother. There a gargantuan feast took place. Here are four recipes the Carters love:

CRANBERRY RING MOLD

- 2   envelopes unflavored gelatin
- ½   cup cold water
- ¾   cup boiling water
- ¼   cup fresh lemon juice
- 2   cans (1 pound each) jellied cranberry sauce
- ½   cup cold water
- ½   teaspoon bottled horseradish
- 2   to 3 dashes liquid red pepper seasoning
- ¼   teaspoon salt
       Apple-Pecan Salad (recipe follows)

In a large mixing bowl, sprinkle gelatin over ½ cup cold water to soften. Add boiling water and stir until the gelatin is dissolved. Stir in lemon juice.

Combine cranberry sauce and ½ cup cold water in a saucepan. Stir, then beat with whisk until it is smooth; do not allow to boil. Add horseradish, hot pepper seasoning, and salt. Stir in gelatin mixture. Pour into a 6-cup ring mold that has been rinsed with cold water. Chill about 4 hours, or until firm. Unmold onto round serving plate. Fill center with apple and pecan salad. Surround with additional salad if desired.

Serves 6 to 8.

NOTE: Miss Allie doubles this recipe to make two ring molds to serve her large family.

Both the ring mold and the salad can be prepared ahead, but the cranberry molds should be unmolded and filled with the salad just before serving.

APPLE-PECAN SALAD FILLING
FOR CRANBERRY MOLDS

2   cups peeled and chopped tart crisp apples
1   teaspoon lemon juice
½   cup thinly sliced celery
1   cup coarsely chopped pecans
¼   cup mayonnaise
¼   teaspoon salt
½   cup heavy cream, whipped

Combine apples, lemon juice, celery, pecans, mayonnaise, and salt; stir to blend. Cover and refrigerate the mixture until about 1 hour before serving. Fold in the whipped cream. Return salad to refrigerator until time to serve.

Makes sufficient salad to fill 2 6-cup cranberry molds, with enough left over to surround each mold with salad.

CHEESE RING

1   pound sharp Cheddar cheese
1½ cups (about 6 ounces) grated pecan halves
2   tablespoons grated onion
2   tablespoons milk
¼   teaspoon black pepper
     Dash cayenne pepper
¼   cup mayonnaise, or sufficient to bind mixture
     Strawberry preserves (optional)

Grate cheese into a large mixing bowl. Add remaining ingredients and cream with a heavy wooden spoon until smooth.

Transfer to a round or oblong platter and with hands pat out flat, leaving a higher rim around edge. Refrigerate until chilled.

When ready to serve, fill center with strawberry preserves if desired.

JAPANESE FRUITCAKE

1   cup (2 sticks) butter, at room temperature

2 cups sugar
4 eggs
3 cups flour
½ teaspoon salt
3 teaspoons baking powder
1 cup milk
1 tablespoon grated orange rind
1 teaspoon vanilla
1 teaspoon allspice
1 teaspoon ginger
½ cup raisins
½ cup chopped pecans
1 tablespoon flour
Fruit Filling (recipe follows)
1½ cups grated coconut
Candied cherries (optional)

Preheat oven to 350° F.

Grease and flour 3 9-inch layer cake pans. Cream butter and sugar with electric mixer until soft and fluffy. Beat eggs until light and add to butter-sugar mixture.

Sift flour, salt, and baking powder together and add alternately to batter with milk. Stir in vanilla and orange rind; beat well. Spread ⅔ of the batter into 2 of the 3 prepared pans.

Add allspice and ginger to remaining batter. Sprinkle 1 tablespoon flour over the raisins and nuts to coat, then add to batter and mix well. Spread spice batter into remaining third pan.

Bake layers at 350° F. for 30 minutes, or until cake tests done and sides shrink from pan. Invert layers on wire rack and let cool.

When layers are completely cool, spread fruit filling between them and thinly over the top and side of cake, using a wide-bladed knife to spread evenly. (Place the fruit/spice layer in the middle when stacking layers.) Cover top and side of cake with the coconut. Decorate with red and green candied cherries in a wreath design if desired.

FRUIT FILLING FOR JAPANESE FRUITCAKE

2 tablespoons flour
Juice of 3 lemons
1 cup sugar
1 can (1 pound 4 ounces) crushed pineapple, drained
2 egg yolks
½ cup chopped pecans

Combine all ingredients in top half of a double boiler over, not in, simmering water and cook, stirring frequently, until mixture thickens. It should be quite thick. Remove from heat and allow to cool, stirring occasionally.

Here are some sample menus from White House Christmases past. They show how Presidents of different eras dined on Christmas Day.

Christmas dinner with the Polks (1845–49) was simple and featured blazing plum pudding.

Oyster Soup

Celery   Turkey   Homemade Wafers

Ham   Spiced Round

Salsify   Caramel Sweet Potatoes

Pickles   Rice   Cranberry Sauce

Blazing Plum Pudding

Wine Jelly   Charlotte Russe

Grapefruit Salad   Fruit Cake

Nuts   Raisins

Wine   Coffee

President Benjamin Harrison's Christmas dinner, 1890, was more elaborate and ended with expensive imported fruits.

Blue Point Oysters, half shell

Consommé Royal

Bouches à la Reine

Turkey   Cranberry Jelly

Potatoes Duchesse   Stewed Celery

Terrapin à la Maryland

Lettuce Salad   Plain Dressing

Mince Pie   American Plum Pudding

Tutti-frutti Ice Cream

Lady-fingers   Macaroons   Carlsbad Wafers

Apples, Florida Oranges, Bananas, Grapes, Pears

Black Coffee

Christmas Day with Grover Cleveland, 1887, began with a hearty breakfast:

Oranges
Boiled Rice
Broiled Salt Mackerel
Poached Eggs À La Crème
Potato Fillets
Feather Griddle Cakes
Wheat Bread
Coffee

Dinner centered around seafood and duckling.

Game Soup

Boiled White Fish		Sauce Maître D'Hôtel
Roast Goose		Apple Sauce
Boiled Potatoes		Mashed Turnips
Creamed Parsnips		Stewed Onions
Boiled Rice		Lobster Salad

Canvas Back Duck

Christmas Plum Pudding   Sauce

Vanilla Ice Cream

Mince Pie	Orange Jelly
Delicate Cake	Salted Almonds
Confectionery	Fruits

Coffee

Supper was light but tasty.

Cold Roast Goose
Oyster Patties
Cole Slaw   Buns
Charlotte Russe
Peach Jelly
Tea

In 1933, the Christmas dinner menu was an elaborate one. It included five courses.

Clam Cocktail		Saltines
	Clear Soup	
	Beaten Biscuit	
Curled Celery		Stuffed Olives
	Filet of Fish	
	Sauce Marechale	
	Sliced Cucumbers	

Rolls
Roast Turkey
Chestnut Dressing
Deerfoot Sausage
Cranberry Jelly
Creamed Onions   Green Beans
Candied Sweet Potatoes
Cheese Straws
Plum Pudding
Hard Sauce
Ice Cream
Small Cakes   Cookies
Coffee
Candy

Of the 1937 dinner, the housekeeper stated: "This was one of the nicest of the White House Christmases, and I served the usual family dinner, and the whole family enjoyed it, including the President [FDR], who seemed like himself again."

Blue Points   Saltines
Calf's Head Soup
Fairy Toast
Curled Celery   Stuffed Olives
Roast Turkey
Sausage   Chestnut Dressing
Cranberry Sauce
Beans   Sweet Potatoes and Apples
Grapefruit Salad
Plum Pudding   Hard Sauce
Ice-Cream Cake   Coffee

A favorite Carter menu was simple, but hearty and featured a special salad.

Relish Tray
Celery hearts, carrot sticks, homemade pickles,
homemade pickled peaches,
and watermelon rind preserves
Roast Turkey
Corn Bread Stuffing
Rice
Turkey Giblet Gravy

85

Candied Sweet Potatoes
Green Beans, New Southern-Style
Cheese Ring Filled with
Strawberry preserves
(Jimmy's all-time favorite)
Cranberry Ring Mold
Filled with Apple-Pecan Salad
Hot Yeast Rolls
Japanese Fruitcake
Ambrosia
Coffee

Most White House Christmas feasts since colonial times have been planned around the traditional American bird, the turkey, and each White House chef has added personal specialties. Many menu items like the Carter corn-bread stuffing reflect regional tastes.

8
Romance

Romance is as much a part of Christmas as plum pudding. Christina Rossetti's poem "Love Came Down at Christmas" tells why:

> "Love came down at Christmas,
>   Love all lovely, Love divine;
> Love was born at Christmas,
>   Star and angels gave the sign."

Human as well as divine love flourishes at this season. Romance first bloomed at the third Christmas of President James Monroe in 1819. His beautiful young daughter, Maria Hester, fell in love with Samuel Gouveneur, her own first cousin. Gouveneur, a New Yorker and for a time private secretary to the President, is said to have whispered "the sweetest story ever told" into Maria's ears at the White House Christmas party. Though scarcely sixteen, she was described as "much traveled, mature for her years, lovably romantic and intensely proud of being the President's daughter." She married Gouveneur in the first White House wedding of a presidential daughter, held a few months after the fateful Christmas meeting.

At the 1831 White House Christmas party, Mary Anne Lewis, daughter of President Andrew Jackson's friend, Major William Lewis, met Alphonse Pageot, a secretary at the French Legation. The eighteen-year-old beauty, who was living at the White House at the time, fell in love with the charming diplomat. In 1832, they were married at the White House in a Catholic ceremony—the first one held at the White House and the only one until the Eisenhower Administration.

A Christmas party at a Mississippi plantation brought Jefferson Davis and Varina Howell together. Their love soon blossomed, and she became the second wife of the ill-fated President of the Confederate States of America.

In 1878 a debutante from Cincinnati, Helen Herron, attended the White House Christmas party. Her father was a friend of President Rutherford B. Hayes. She boasted that she would return one day. She did. In 1909 she took up residence as First Lady of the Land, Mrs. William Howard Taft.

But the grandest romance of all resulted in a Christmas wedding and honeymoon in 1915 for Woodrow Wilson and Edith Bolling Galt. The grief-stricken Mr. Wilson, who had lost his wife, Ellen, the year before, met the charming widow of a banker on a March day in 1915 when she stepped out of the elevator on the second floor of the White House. She was clad in a walking outfit and her boots were splashed with mud when she unexpectedly encountered the President. Mrs. Galt was a friend of Admiral Cary Grayson, the President's physician. She and the widowed President were drawn almost inexorably to each other by virtue of common interests and upbringing. Their courtship was ardent, intense, and brief.

Both loved theater, golf, baseball, quiet dinners, and evening drives along blossom-scented roads. By October they were ready to announce their engagement and impending marriage.

The President did not want to wait. He needed Edith. His advisers warned of the political consequences, for the 1916 campaign would soon be upon them. Already, hostile criticism of the "merry widower" in the White House was escalating throughout the land, even in the President's native Southland. A marriage so soon after his first wife's death was considered politically unthinkable. But the stubborn scholar-President was adamant. He and Edith were to be married at her home just before Christmas.

The Wilsons' wedding day, December 18, was blustery and rainy. A driving rain had fallen in torrents all during the night. Gusty winds blew in the morning as caterers, florists, and Secret Service men descended upon the modest red-brick townhouse at 1318 20th Street in Washington. Then, about noon, the sun came out, pronouncing its blessing on this special day.

All day long curious people lingered near the residence. Hundreds of motorcars detoured to catch a glimpse of the day's proceedings. Photographers and policemen were everywhere.

88

Illustrated Weekly Newspaper

Dec 23rd 1915   *Established in 1855*   Price 10 Cents

*A magazine cover celebrated the Wilson-Galt
Christmas wedding*

Christmas decorations and evergreens graced the houses.

By early evening the guests had begun to arrive. Attired in evening dress, they came in motorcars and in horse-drawn carriages. Just before 8 P.M. the President's limousine arrived.

The ceremony was simple and impressive. It was jointly conducted by Rev. Herbert Scott Smith, rector of St. John's Episcopal Church, the bride's pastor and a former student of the President's, and Rev. James H. Taylor, pastor of Central Presbyterian Church, the President's church. The Episcopal bishop of Washington was

89

to have officiated, but his arrogance offended Mrs. Galt and she dismissed him!

The President was spiffily attired in evening clothes. Mrs. Galt wore a black-velvet gown and matching hat, tilted at a fetching angle. She wore a diamond brooch, a gift from her betrothed. The couple took their vows under a canopy of greenery, shell-shaped and lined with heather, symbolic of the President's Scottish heritage. The room was scented with banks of crimson roses and mauve orchids and lighted by candles. The bride and groom knelt on a white satin prie-dieu.

The house was bedecked with flowers, particularly orchids and roses. A string orchestra, hidden behind the ferns, played romantic music. An elegant supper followed the ceremony.

The President and his new bride, desirous of privacy, concocted a little getaway scheme to fool the press and the crowd of onlookers. Instead of boarding the honeymoon train at Washington's Union Station or at Alexandria station, the party zigzagged around the city in an attempt to lose ten press cars that were in hot pursuit. They were successful. The night had turned cold and beautiful, with a gently falling snow. In her autobiography, *My Memoir*, Mrs. Wilson recalled, "We had a lovely drive over in the moonlight with the world lying white with snow around us."

The bride and groom boarded their private pullman car on a siding close to the Alexandria freightyard. They were bound for Hot Springs, a secluded and elegant resort in western Virginia. The crowds had been eluded. Now the President could be alone with his bride for the ten-hour journey. Only Colonel Starling of the Secret Service was with them.

Starling's memoirs, published some years later, include a piquant story. The Secret Service man relates that he discreetly entered the President's car the next morning to see if all was well. The scene he encountered was etched on his memory.

The nation's stuffy, scholarly President was dancing a jig and singing a popular tune. The President, "clad in top hat, tailcoat and grey morning trousers, was clicking his heels and singing 'Oh, you beautiful doll, you great big beautiful doll.' "

The Wilsons were supremely happy at Hot Springs, where an entire wing at the Homestead Hotel had been given to them (and to the ubiquitous Secret Service). They golfed, dined leisurely, and took long drives in the snow-clad countryside.

Like most honeymooners, the Wilsons kept to themselves for

the first week. On Christmas Eve a large tree was decorated in their honor in the private dining room. The couple made their first public appearance in the lobby at 9 P.M. The several hundred guests gave them a standing tribute. A group of black singers provided appropriately festive music.

On Christmas, the Wilsons breakfasted in their private suite, which had been festooned with holly and evergreens. The manager sent them a miniature Christmas tree decorated with crystal and tinsel ornaments and tiny colored electric bulbs. Upon the topmost branch reposed a dove of peace.

Boxes of roses and orchids arrived from the White House, along with candies and hundreds of Christmas messages and telegrams. Packages arrived by express all day long. The common people of America had been deeply moved by the President's newfound love. They expressed their admiration by inundating the couple with messages and gifts.

At midday the Wilsons played a game of golf until they were rained out at the fourteenth hole.

They were served tea in the afternoon and an elaborate Christmas dinner in the evening.

On December 26, the Wilsons insisted on their daily drive in the President's Pierce Arrow, despite the foot of snow on the ground. On the twenty-eighth the President celebrated his fifty-ninth birthday.

This magic world soon came to an end. Bad news from the war in Europe compelled them to cut short their planned stay. They hurried back to the White House on January 3, 1916.

9
Going Away for Christmas

During most of the nineteenth century, Presidents preferred to stay in their official residence at 1600 Pennsylvania Avenue for the holidays, though Jefferson and Madison sorely missed their Virginia plantations. From 1901 on, Teddy Roosevelt tried to get home to Oyster Bay or to his Virginia hunting lodge for a portion of the festive season, but he was not always able to do so.

One of the first presidential Christmas holiday trips was Woodrow Wilson's 1913 visit to Pass Christian, Mississippi, a lovely Gulf Coast town with a French heritage.

Rear Admiral Cary T. Grayson, the President's solicitous physician, was always concerned for the First Family's health and well-being. It was he who devised "an innocent intrigue" to convince the Wilsons to spend a few days in the warm climate of the Gulf Coast. Pass Christian was "a sleepy little place on the Gulf of Mexico," according to Wilson's daughter Eleanor, but it was considered ideal for playing golf and motoring by the water. So, after coping with pressing congressional business, the President and his party left Washington on December 23.

Eleanor Wilson McAdoo, in her memoirs, *The Woodrow Wilsons,* remembered that delightful Christmas: "The house at Pass Christian had been built before the Civil War. I felt as though we had been suddenly transported to the faraway days at Colonel Stribling's; there were the same tall white columns, romantic balconies, soft-voiced Negro servants and the gentle consideration of the neighbors. But here the garden was a mass of luxuriant bloom, the trees festooned with moss and, riding through the woods, we were constantly coming upon little winding rivers and still green bayous.

"On Christmas morning we had a big tree, but it seemed

strangely out of place with warm sun streaming through the windows, and we spent the rest of the day picnicking."

Admiral Grayson remembered several "amusing incidents" of this Christmas vacation:

"One day while the President and I were returning to Pass Christian from Gulfport where we had been playing golf, a little boy about ten years of age stood in the middle of the road, and with the motions of a traffic cop, waved our automobile to a stop. It turned out that he had some oranges which he wanted to give the President. The President accepted the humble offering with thanks, asked the boy where he lived, told him to climb into the car, and drove the child to his home. The next day the President wrote him a nice letter of appreciation. A few days afterward while coming along this road the little boy waved us down again. He did not have a basket this time, but he told the President that he enjoyed the letter so much that he would like to have the President write him every week after he got back to Washington. The President was very much pleased over this little incident."

The President of the United States even helped to extinguish a fire at a neighbor's house. Wrote Admiral Grayson: "We were returning another day from the golf course when he noticed smoke curling up from the roof of a residence. We ran to the door and knocked and were received by the lady of the house with flutterings of excitement. 'Oh, Mr. President,' she exclaimed, 'it is so good of you to call on me. Won't you please walk into the parlor and sit down?' To which the President replied: 'I haven't time to sit down—your house is on fire.'

"We formed a bucket brigade but the lady in her double excitement was so confused that she seized a pitcher without any water in it. Climbing through the garret to the roof we extinguished the fire and in recognition of our prowess both the President and I were elected members of the Pass Christian Fire Department."

The President attended services at a local Presbyterian church, whose pastor was obviously a Republican. The elderly minister told the President, "This is the second greatest honor that ever came into my life." Wilson seemed taken aback, but did not inquire further.

Grayson, however, pressed the point, whereupon the minister replied that President Grant had once attended services in his church. Still, the President seemed amused and asked for a copy

93

of the hymnal, which was similar to the one he had used as a child growing up in a Presbyterian manse. This ancient and rather weather-beaten hymnal was used by the President at Sunday evening hymn-singing sessions in the Oval Room of the White House.

President Wilson spent Christmas away from the White House in 1918, when he was making his grand triumphal tour of Europe, where he was hailed as a conquering hero. He and his second wife, Edith, spent Christmas with U.S. troops in France. On December 22, a Sunday, the Wilsons visited a hospital of French soldiers, where a moving incident transpired. Mrs. Wilson told the story in her autobiography:

"When we had finished the dreary round of the wards, we were asked to come into the main room to see some of the convalescent patients who were having a little Christmas celebration. I wish I knew how to draw with my pen the scene in that room so you could see it as I do. It is as vivid today, twenty years later, as it was that Sunday, December 22, 1918! A low-ceilinged room, whitewashed walls, a cheap upright piano almost the only furniture; men in the blue French uniform standing close as they could be packed, many leaning on crutches or with bandages around their eyes, or shattered arms in slings; the whole lighted from one tiny bulb, dropped by a cord from the ceiling over which was a small bit of red paper and a French flag. Leaning against the piano was a big poilu with both eyes gone, just empty sockets, and a slender pallid boy with one leg was striking the keys in the accompaniment to the 'Marseillaise.' The big blind fellow in blue, wearing on his breast the Croix de guerre, was the only one who sang. It was one of the most dramatic moments of my life, for God seemed to have given him a voice in place of eyes. Its tones were so mellow that 'only in Heaven shall I hear that chord again.' There were tears in it—tears which had dropped from those sockets where eyes should have been; tears for all the suffering of his dear torn country under whose tiny flag he sang triumphant."

The President was busy with official business on the twenty-third and twenty-fourth, but still managed to slip away and do some Christmas shopping in Paris. He bought books at Brentano's on the Rue de la Paix, gloves at Perines on the Avenue de l'Opera, and flowers at the open-air flower stall near the Madeleine.

At midnight on Christmas Eve, the Wilsons left for General Pershing's headquarters at Chaumont by a special train provided by the President of France. There was no heat. The sleeping compartments were "as cold as vaults," said Edith Wilson, and the French Ambassador to the United States indignantly lamented the state of affairs.

The living conditions of the U.S. troops were deplorable. Mud, snow, and ice surrounded the temporary shacks and the canteen, where the lonely soldiers had made a pitiful attempt to decorate for Christmas with a few greens and little bits of red paper.

The troops tried to bring Christmas cheer to the Wilsons. Mrs. Wilson recalled the great Christmas dinner:

"It was a real traditional American dinner, with turkey, cranberry sauce, and pumpkin pie cut army fashion in slices large as this page, and plenty for each to have an encore if he wanted one. General Leorat, who was beside me, said he had heard of this pie but never seen it before. He looked dubiously at the great yellow square before him. Compared with French pastry, it was a little formidable looking, so I watched his approach to it. A very conservative corner morsel was his first and last tribute to good U.S.A. pumpkin pie. It was a merry meal with good stories and high spirits, and we were sorry to say goodbye to the boys when the time came.

"Again we had a long drive to General Pershing's chateau where he and his staff lived. As we were all frozen to the marrow it was comforting to find open fires and steaming hot tea ready for us in this spacious house. We stayed long enough to thaw out and get an idea of the place and of the personnel of the General's staff, and at dark went again to the train for another night trip back to Paris."

One of the most widely reported presidential holidays was the Calvin Coolidges' 1928 visit to Sapelo Island, Georgia. This secluded island is part of Georgia's fabled Golden Isles, steeped in history.

Pirates, Jesuit and Anglican missionaries, and wars between the Spanish and the English are part of the colorful history of Georgia's Atlantic seacoast. The eighteenth-century "War of Jenkins Ear" was fought in this area. John Wesley was a young Anglican missionary preacher for about a year here in the 1740s. Historic Episcopal and Catholic chapels dot the area. Christ Church in Frederica welcomed President and Mrs. Coolidge in the closing days of his presidency.

At that time, the Golden Isles were truly unspoiled and lightly populated. Many of the local residents were fisherfolk who had

*The Trumans' 1946 greeting shows them ready
to take off for Independence*

never left the area in their lives.

The Coolidges stayed at the mansion-estate of Howard Coffin of Detroit, a retired automobile engineer and a member of the President's aviation board. His estate had once been a rendezvous of buccaneers. A ruined Spanish mission stood nearby, amid the moss-covered trees and poinsettias.

It was truly a jubilant vacation for the normally taciturn and sober President. He even insisted on taking the entire White House domestic staff with him on the special train that left Washington at 3 P.M. on Christmas Day.

96

A famous British portrait painter, Frank O. Salisbury, accompanied the party. He was commissioned to paint the portraits of the President and the First Lady. Salisbury had painted King George V's portrait and was later to paint two other American Presidents.

Salisbury remembered his Christmas adventure with great relish. He wrote: "I have had the good fortune to paint three American Presidents, beginning with President Coolidge. It was my first visit to Washington, a romantic experience. I had come by the night train from New York on Christmas Eve, and the crisp dawn lent enchantment to the beautiful city dominated by a dome which sets an Englishman thinking of St. Paul's. I was braced with expectancy and enthusiasm for the adventure of this visit to the White House.

"The President's car came to meet me, and I was taken to the suite of rooms for visitors, where, after breakfast, the secretary came to say that the President would be ready to receive me at ten o'clock. He asked if I had brought two canvasses, and I said I always carried an extra one. It was customary, he told me, for the artist who painted the President to paint his wife also.

"The usher came at the appointed time and took me down to the President. He was very kind, offering me a cigar. On my explaining that I did not smoke, he said, 'Well, there is very little in these days that we can offer you,' for it was during Prohibition. There was a dish of fruit on the table from which he took an apple and pared it, cutting it in two, and offering me the top half. He took me round the White House, showing me the pictures. On the first landing were two bust portraits, one of Mrs. Coolidge and one of the President, which had just been painted. They were rather caricatures, and the President explained that the artist had insisted on his saying with a snarl every few minutes, 'Tiger! Tiger!' It seemed to me a wild idea, and surely the last thing in the world to express the character of Calvin Coolidge, the silent man. He introduced me to Mrs. Coolidge, whose charming personality and gracious smile had won all hearts. After this I was driven round Washington to see the city."

The Coolidges and their party fell in love with Georgia. The President and his male staffers got up at three in the morning to go hunting for pheasants, wild turkeys, and wild ducks. The President bagged two wild turkeys and three pheasants. On the moss-hung roads where pirates and Spanish missionaries had once meandered, the party encountered wild peacocks and deer. An ancient black guide, "Old Pete," personally led the Chief Executive through the dense thickets, some of which were "untouched by the hand of man," as a national correspondent put it. Coolidge was rarely in so relaxed and jovial a manner. He proudly carried his game into the house. Later in the day, he and the First Lady went sightseeing among the live oak and holly trees, took boat rides in the swamp, and ended up on White Beach, where a majestic sunset was the chief attraction.

A couple of days later the President viewed a unique rodeo in which local blacks rode wild steers bareback. He rode in a native ox cart, and failed to shoot a deer. The President was caparisoned in a ten-gallon hat, hunting boots, and a leather coat.

The rodeo was quite a treat. About one hundred local blacks serenaded the party with spirituals. Oxen, horses, and diamondback turtles were raced. Mrs. Coolidge made moving pictures of the scene.

On another day, the presidential party visited Sea Island and the fashionable Cloisters hotel. Each day the First Couple sat for their portraits. Even though this was the Democratic Deep South, the Coolidges were warmly welcomed wherever they went. Virtually the entire population of Brunswick greeted the presidential train when it entered the palm-studded avenues of the quiet and graceful town. Mrs. Coolidge was clad in furs, which she quickly discarded in the warm sunshine. She brought with her the favorite dog, Tiny Tim, a red chow. Mr. Coolidge expressed delight at the palmettos, the Spanish moss, the live oak trees, and olive groves found in the semitropical region. And a yacht trip through the picturesque inlets delighted everyone. It was with reluctance that the party returned to Washington at the New Year—to begin the transition to the Hoover Administration.

The Hoovers went to Panama for Christmas in 1932, but maintained complete privacy. The Franklin Roosevelts spent all their Christmases but one in the White House. In 1944 a weary FDR dearly wanted to spend a Christmas at home in his beloved Hyde Park. For him, as for many other Presidents, "going away" for Christmas often meant "going home" to the permanent residence.

The Trumans continued this custom by spending all but two of their Christmases at Independence, Missouri. There, on one frigid night, a group of carolers serenaded the President on his front porch. The Eisenhowers spent their first two Christmases, 1953 and 1954, at Augusta, Georgia, enjoying the mild climate and the fine golfing facilities. In 1959, Ike and Mamie stayed at the White House for Christmas Day, but then drove to Gettysburg to see their four grandchildren on the twenty-sixth. Icy highways had prevented their going the day before. Afterward they flew to Augusta. The Kennedys spent their two Christmases in Palm Beach. The Johnsons spent four of their six Christmases at their Texas ranch. The Fords went skiing in Vail, Colorado, and the Carters always returned to their beloved Plains, Georgia.

WASHINGTON D.C. 1798

WHITE HOUSE CHRISTMAS CARDS

On facing page:
The Trumans used a photo. Watercolors commissioned by the Eisenhowers and the Johnsons show views of two facades

On this page:
An N. C. Wyeth painting, an 1831 print, and an 1860 watercolor show, on recent greetings, the White House as it looked over a century ago

THE PRESIDENT'S HOUSE, WASHINGTON.

The President's House, Washington   by Lefevre Cranstone 1860

10

A Greeting from the President

A greeting from the President is a quite recent phenomenon. The Franklin Roosevelts were the first to send out cards from the White House on any large-scale basis. At the request of Mrs. Roosevelt, the White House engraver, Tolly, prepared by hand lithographs of the executive mansion. But these were "personal," or "unofficial," greetings to friends.

It was not until the Eisenhower Administration that "official" cards were sent as a matter of policy to all heads of state, to Cabinet members, to heads of government departments, and to members of Congress.

Card themes have generally been chosen from art works in the White House collection or have been especially commissioned from contemporary artists. A snow-clad White House has been a particular favorite of several Presidents.

The Eisenhowers and Kennedys had separate cards for their personal friends.

In 1962, Mrs. Kennedy selected a photo of a sleigh carrying the children, Caroline and John John, and herself across the South Lawn. The sleigh was pulled by Macaroni, Caroline's pony.

In 1964 the Johnsons chose only one card to be used for both official and personal use. The outdoor scene was a watercolor of their daughters, Lynda and Luci, playing with two beagles in front of the White House. In the foreground were two oak trees planted by the President and Mrs. Johnson near the President's office.

The Nixons selected such scenes as *The President's House from the River 1839,* an N. C. Wyeth painting entitled *Building the First White House,* and an embossed image of the White House prepared by Hallmark Cards. In 1969 the Nixons mailed out 37,000 Christmas cards. The Nixons' list included friends from

102

public and private life, as well as a broad cross section of prominent Americans.

The Fords and the Carters selected engravings of nineteenth-century drawings and photographs from the White House art collection. The Carters mailed more than 100,000 cards in 1980, addressed by a thousand volunteers.

The Reagans selected a particularly beautiful and impressive card for 1981. It was an aqueous paint sketch by Jamie Wyeth, depicting the White House on a snowy, starlit night.

11

A Quiet Christmas

Oh, for a quiet Christmas! How often has that sentiment echoed throughout American homes. For a number of our Presidents quiet has been the desired mood.

Several newspaper headlines reflect this tranquil spirit: "Coolidges Spend a Quiet Christmas," "Holiday Is Quiet for Eisenhowers," "Hoovers Plan Quiet Holiday with Son," "President Stays at Home." Even some of our most energetic Presidents sought an occasional Christmas of peace and quiet. In 1917 *The New York Times* reported: "Quiet ceremonies, few in number, marked the celebration of Washington's first war Christmas. The President and Mrs. Wilson remained at home all day." Margaret Truman wrote of the 1948 holiday: "Christmas was quiet that year. It was a family time."

Most of the nineteenth-century Presidents adhered to a very quiet, personal family time at Christmas. Decorations and formal activities were minimal, and the press respected the First Family's desire for privacy.

An example of a quiet man was James K. Polk, an early nineteenth-century version of today's workaholic. He literally worked himself to death in the White House, dying only three months after leaving the presidency in 1849. His conscientiousness and diligent attention to duty had hastened his death.

He was unable to relax and considered social activities vain, superfluous, and perhaps a little wicked. It is hardly surprising that White House social life under the childless Polks was stilted, formal, and not a little grim, though there were numerous formal parties.

His wife, Sarah, resolutely refused to serve wine or "spirituous liquors" at White House dinners, no matter how gala the occasion.

104

*A December Sunday in 1886 found the Grover
Clevelands at the First Presbyterian Church*

It was she, rather than "Lemonade Lucy" Hayes thirty years later,
who first brought prohibition to the President's House. One account, however, claims that wine was served at least once at a
White House dinner.

The Polks were sobersided and dull. Historian Allan Nevins,
in his introduction to Polk's diary of his presidency, noted:

"His range of interests was remarkably limited, and his mind
strikes us as rather arid and inelastic. Did he ever read a novel in
his life, or attend a nineteenth-century play, or read any modern
poetry? If so, the evidence is not here. Did he know anything of

105

art, of music, or of nature, or care to know anything about them? From his diary and other papers no one would suspect that he did. We are told that Mrs. Polk, an attractive woman of great dignity and a strict Presbyterian (Polk himself belonged to no church and preferred the Methodist denomination), shunned what she looked upon as 'the vanities of the world,' and that she would not permit dancing in the White House."

The Polks took little note of Christmas. In his diary for December 23 and 24, 1845, Polk described several routine political meetings, but did not acknowledge any seasonal references. For December 25 of that year, he took a rather Scrooge-like approach to the holiday, saying: "This being Christmas Day no company called, with a very few exceptions who remained but for a short time. Congress had adjourned, the public offices were closed, and no public business was transacted."

On Christmas Eve 1846, though, Polk told his diary: "I had a dinner party today. Between thirty and forty persons, members of the two houses of Congress and several ladies of their families, dined with me."

For Christmas Day he wrote: "Not more than half a dozen persons called today, and they were on business. It being Christmas Day, the family attended church. I remained in my office, attended to some of the business on my table, and wrote a rough draft of a message which I have made up my mind to send to Congress."

The impression conveyed is that of a man almost totally impervious to social niceties or to the festive spirit of the Christmas season.

As a general rule, Zachary Taylor, Martin Van Buren, Franklin Pierce, James Buchanan, and Andrew Johnson spent their holidays in tranquillity. Rutherford and Lucy Hayes tried to preserve a peaceful atmosphere within a festive setting. They loved dignified dinners, receptions, and hymn-singing sessions around the piano in the parlor, which Mrs. Hayes played. "The President and Mrs. Hayes spent a quiet but much-enjoyed Christmas at the Executive Mansion today," commented the *New York Tribune* in 1880.

The Grover Cleveland Christmases centered around church services.

Both of the Harding Christmases were uneventful. In 1921 the Hardings had no overnight guests. Since they were childless, they dined alone at all three meals. After attending services at

106

Calvary Baptist Church, they opened presents and read postcards sent by admirers. In 1922 the press reported that the President "would hang up his stocking at home and, with the possible exception of attending church that Sunday, nothing would break the quietude of the holiday." The Hardings dined on a huge turkey given to them at Thanksgiving. The gobbler had been fattened by White House guards for several weeks so that it would be good and ready for the holiday feast.

Christmas at the White House in 1927 was a very quiet affair. Mr. Coolidge arose early, opened a few presents, attended church, dined early, and then worked on business for several hours. There was no celebration and no callers. Only his son John was home from college. The Hoovers celebrated most of their Christmases quietly and without fanfare.

The pressing demands of the job often intruded on the President's Christmas. Lady Bird Johnson often complained that Lyndon was constantly on the telephone during the holiday season. Mr. Eisenhower spent several hours in his office on Christmas Day in 1960. In 1919 a convalescing Woodrow Wilson signed a foreign trade bill on Christmas. Then he rested in the White House garden, ate his dinner in his room, and read the large number of Christmas messages that he received from all parts of the world.

The death of a loved one has also contributed to the quietness of the holiday. For Woodrow Wilson in 1914 this was poignantly clear. His beloved wife of twenty-nine years, Ellen, had died the previous summer. His grief had turned to despondency, and his personal physician, Admiral Cary Grayson, was concerned for the President's health. Still, as Christmas approached, Wilson decided to honor his wife's memory by trying to carry on in the usual manner.

President Wilson insisted on having a grand tree in the White House library on the second floor for his granddaughter Nancy McAdoo and his grandniece Anne Cochron. He decorated it with his own hands and played the role of Santa Claus, to the infinite delight of the two youngsters.

All three of his daughters and their families helped the lonely Chief Executive celebrate that first Christmas without Ellen. On Christmas Day the President played golf at the Washington Country Club in Arlington, but skipped church services at Central Presbyterian Church.

Illness as well as bereavement affected celebration. In 1892,

107

Benjamin Harrison struggled to keep joy in a saddened White House. His beloved wife had died a few days before Election Day. Mr. Harrison had been defeated for reelection. His entire Administration had, in fact, been overshadowed by personal tragedies and deaths among staff and Cabinet members. To top it all off, the lonely President's granddaughter came down with scarlet fever, and the White House had to be quarantined all through the holidays. But the President insisted on climbing a ladder to help workmen put up and decorate the tree.

This tradition of carrying on despite personal loss can be seen in the 1924 Christmas. Calvin and Grace Coolidge had lost their younger son, Calvin, Jr., the previous summer, when blood poisoning developed from a blister on the lad's foot after a game of tennis. The sixteen-year-old boy was dead in a matter of days. As Christmas approached, Mrs. Coolidge wrote a friend: "I shall not be sad at this happy time of year. I shall have the Christmas carols this year as I did last, out on the North Portico."

In the case of the McKinleys, the approach of Christmas always brought on sad memories, for their first child, Katherine, had been born on Christmas Day in 1871 but had died in 1876. Another child had also died in infancy.

Margaret Leech tells how the memories of the past impinged on the Christmas of 1899: "The holiday season was always saddened by memories of little Katie, who had been born on Christmas Day. This year, McKinley seemed more than usually solemn, as the wreaths were hung in the hushed and unfrequented mansion."

Mrs. McKinley loved diamonds. The President had given her two diamond bracelets for Christmas in 1898. But he had to confess in 1899, " 'I don't know what in the world to give Mrs. McKinley for Christmas.'

"William Sinclair, a mulatto manservant and valet to McKinley, settled the question of Christmas. He went to Galt's jewelry store and brought back a beautiful vase and an exquisite little blue picture frame, set with jewels. The President put Katie's photograph in the frame, and Mrs. McKinley was 'delighted' with the pretty enshrinement of their sorrow."

Other December deaths in the First Family include Grant's father-in-law, who died in 1873, and Truman's mother-in-law, who died in 1952. And both Abraham Lincoln and Jefferson Davis lost young sons during the Civil War, tragedies which cast a pall over their Christmas celebrations.

For Jefferson Davis, the last Christmas of the Confederacy was noted for its hunger, sorrow, and suffering. There was little food. There was even less hope. In Richmond, the occupants of the Confederate White House tried their best to honor the birth of Christ in a time of dismay and impending doom.

Richmond residents were hungry and cold. The sound of guns could be heard in the distance. On Christmas Eve, the North rejoiced over General Sherman's message to Abraham Lincoln: "I beg to present you as a Christmas present the city of Savannah, with 150 heavy guns and plenty of ammunition, and also about 25,000 bales of cotton." For the South, the end was fast approaching.

With the true grit of a courageous southern woman, Mrs. Varina Davis was determined to keep Christmas in the old way. The family rations had shrunk to rice, cornmeal, and an occasional piece of meat. Several generous donors had sent her rice, flour, molasses, and meat, which she distributed to the needy. She personally took food, makeshift toys, and sweets to poor children and to orphans at a church-run orphanage.

She urged her friends to contribute old toys. Her own children gathered up their unused toys and clothing for the less fortunate. A black servant, Robert Brown, made an exquisite dollhouse. Varina's mother made pillows, mattresses, and sheets. Other residents of the Confederate White House went to work to spruce up the mansion for Christmas.

On Christmas Eve, young people came in to string apples and popcorn for the tree. A neighbor sent candles. An Italian immigrant gave candy. A tree was erected at nearby St. Paul's Episcopal Church, where the family worshiped. On Christmas Day, President Davis helped to distribute gifts.

Varina managed to find some substitute ingredients so the family could enjoy traditional mince pie and plum pudding. All the servants wished the President and his First Lady a Merry Christmas, and all were given small gifts.

The family's stockings had been stuffed with molasses candy, apples, woolen gloves, paper dolls, and small tops. The President received a pair of chamois-skin riding gauntlets. Varina's gifts included six cakes of soap, some homespun linen thread, a pincushion, a book of Swinburne's poems, and a needlebook.

The Davises then walked to St. Paul's for Christmas services and visited the orphans. General Robert E. Lee called at the Confederate White House while they were gone to thank them for a barrel of sweet potatoes he had received (by mistake!). Lee had taken a small dishful of that favorite southern dish and had given the rest to his starving soldiers.

The day ended with a party. Brave and gallant officers, knowing that the cause for which they labored was soon to end, put on their dress uniforms and danced to war tunes and Christmas carols.

12
The President Speaks

What the President says on just about any topic is usually noticed. On the subject of Christmas, we find little in the public record until 1891, when Benjamin Harrison spoke to a New York journalist about the religious and social meaning of the holiday. The President not only called Christmas "the most sacred religious festival of the year" but commented at length on the manner in which most Americans then celebrated the holiday. Here is the President's statement:

"Christmas is the most sacred religious festival of the year, and should be an occasion of general rejoicing throughout the land, from the humblest citizen to the highest official, who, for the time being, should forget or put behind him his cares and annoyances, and participate in the spirit of seasonable festivity. We intend to make it a happy day at the White House—all the members of my family, representing four generations, will gather around the big table in the State dining room to have an old-fashioned Christmas dinner. Besides Mrs. Harrison, there will be her father, Dr. Scott, Mr. and Mrs. M'Kee and their children, Mrs. Dimmick and Lieutenant and Mrs. Parker. I am an ardent believer in the duty we owe to ourselves as Christians to make merry for children at Christmas time, and we shall have an old-fashioned Christmas tree for the grandchildren upstairs; and I shall be their Santa Claus myself. If my influence goes for aught in this busy world, let me hope that my example may be followed in every family in the land.

"Christmas is made as much of in this country as it is in England, if not more. The plum-pudding is not universal, but the Christmas tree is in almost every home. Even in the tenement districts of the East side, inhabited by the labouring and poorer classes, these vernal emblems of the anniversary are quite as much in demand as in other quarters, and if they and the gifts hung upon them are less elaborate than our West side congeners, the household enthusiasm which welcomes them is quite as marked. As in London, the streets are flooded with Christmas numbers of the periodicals, which, it may be remarked, are this year more elaborate in design and execution than ever. The use of Christmas cards has also obtained surprising proportions. A marked feature of this year's Christmas is the variety and elegance of offerings after the Paris fashion, which are of a purely ornamental and but slight utilitarian character. There are bonbonnières in a variety of forms, some of them very magnificent and expensive; while the Christmas cards range in price from a cent to ten dollars each. These bonbonnières, decked with expensive ribbon or hand-painted with designs of the season, attain prices as high as forty dollars each, and are in great favour among the wealthy classes. Flowers are also much used, and, just now, are exceedingly costly.

"While the usual religious ceremonies of the day are generally observed here, the mass of the community are inclined to treat the occasion as a festive rather than a solemn occasion, and upon festivity the whole population at the present time seems bent."

In 1899, President McKinley's secretary George Cortelyou recorded in his diary this sober reflection from the President: "One should feel *holy* at this season, the time should be one of resolution and reflection; the spirit of self-sacrifice should dominate everything."

It remained for Calvin Coolidge to initiate the custom of a formal presidential statement at Christmas. Just as the first lighting of the National Christmas Tree was begun by Coolidge in 1923, so was the presidential Christmas message. In 1925 he issued a message to the nation's disabled veterans, saying: "I take great pleasure in sending my holiday greetings to you who have sacrificed so much in order to maintain the honor of our country.

"America will never forget the unselfish services of those who have rallied to her defense. Particularly does the heart of the nation go out to those whose health and strength were impaired as a result of your devotion.

"Our Government will continue its solicitous care of those seeking restoration and rehabilitation. Nothing possible in that direction will be left undone. I need scarcely dwell on this. But, most of all, I want you to understand how fully you have the

112

gratitude and sympathy of your fellow citizens in the gallant struggle you are making against ill-health and disability.

"May this season bring to you good cheer in abundance, and may the coming year be filled with happiness."

In 1927 he issued a Christmas message "to the American people." It was terse but evocative of the true meaning of Christmas. Mr. Coolidge said: "Christmas is not a time or a season, but a state of mind. To cherish peace and good will, to be plenteous in mercy is to have the real spirit of Christmas. If we think on these things, there will be born in us a Savior and over us will shine a star sending its gleam of hope to the world."

Herbert Hoover was a man of few words. His Christmas messages were brief and rather ethereal. Here, for example, is his 1932 message to the nation's Christmas Tree Association in Fresno, California:

"Your Christmas service held each year at the foot of a living tree which was alive at the time of the birth of Christ, has now for several years lent an inspiring note to the celebration of Christmas. It should be continued as a further symbol of the unbroken chain of life leading back to this great moment in the spiritual life of mankind."

By contrast, Franklin D. Roosevelt, the great communicator, made his messages warm and earthy. He made his audiences feel that he cared about them personally, despite depressions and wars. When World War II came, FDR let Americans know that his sons were fighting abroad, just like their sons. He and Eleanor missed them. Christmas would not quite be Christmas until all family members were reunited.

One of the most eloquent presidential Christmas messages was FDR's last, that of Christmas Eve, 1944. He said:

"It is not easy to say 'Merry Christmas' to you, my fellow Americans, in this time of destructive war. Nor can I say 'Merry Christmas' lightly tonight to our Armed Forces at their battle stations all over the world—or to our allies who fight by their side.

"Here, at home, we will celebrate this Christmas Day in our traditional American way—because of its deep spiritual meaning to us; because the teachings of Christ are fundamental in our lives; and because we want our youngest generation to grow up knowing the significance of this tradition and the story of the coming of the immortal Prince of Peace and Good Will. But, in perhaps every home in the United States, sad and anxious thoughts will be

113

Bess, Harry, and Margaret Truman just before his 1952 Christmas address

continually with the millions of our loved ones who are suffering hardships and misery, and who are risking their very lives to preserve for us and for all mankind the fruits of His teachings and the foundations of civilization itself.

"The Christmas spirit lives tonight in the bitter cold of the front lines in Europe and in the heat of the jungles and swamps of Burma and the Pacific islands. Even the roar of our bombers and fighters in the air and the guns of our ships at sea will not drown out the messages of Christmas which come to the hearts of our fighting men. The thoughts of these men tonight will turn to us here at home around our Christmas trees, surrounded by our children and grandchildren and their Christmas stockings and gifts—just as our own thoughts go out to them, tonight and every night, in their distant places."

The Chief Executive pledged that "Christmases such as those we have known in these years of world tragedy shall not come again to beset the souls of the children of God." He prayed that "God will protect our gallant men and women" . . . and that "He will receive unto His infinite grace those who make their supreme sacrifice in the cause of righteousness, in the cause of love of Him and His teachings." It was an unapologetically religious statement.

FDR's successor, Harry Truman, was also unashamedly religious in many of his Christmas messages. In an increasingly secular age, he was not afraid to proclaim Jesus "the Redeemer of the World" in his 1951 address. Nor did he hesitate to affirm in 1952, his last Christmas at the White House: "Through Jesus Christ the world will yet be a better and a finer place. This faith sustains us today as it has sustained mankind for centuries past. This is why the Christmas story, with the bright stars shining and the angels singing, moves us to wonder and stirs our hearts to praise." He concluded his Christmas message with these words: "I wish for all of you a Christmas filled with the joy of the Holy Spirit, and many years of future happiness with the peace of God reigning upon this earth."

Mr. Truman seemed to relish the preacher role in his Christmas messages. Also in 1952 he said: "The first Christmas was God's great gift to us. This is a wonderful story. Year after year it brings peace and tranquillity to troubled hearts in a troubled world. . . . As we go about our business of trying to achieve peace in the world, let us remember always to try to act and live in the spirit of the Prince of Peace."

Like his predecessor, Truman sought to link the Christmas promise of peace and good will to U.S. military efforts abroad. In 1951, he said: "Our hearts are saddened on this Christmas Eve by the suffering and the sacrifice of our brave men and women in Korea. They are protecting us, and all free men, from aggression. They are trying to prevent another world war."

That same year, Mr. Truman also expressed a sentiment shared by millions of his fellow countrymen: "Christmas is the great home festival. It is the day in all the year which turns our thoughts toward home. And so I am spending Christmas in my old home in Independence with my family and friends."

Dwight Eisenhower also waxed eloquent at Christmastide. And he had a practical side. His holiday remarks were often directed toward particular needs of particular segments of society.

In his last Christmas message in 1960, Ike issued an appeal to holiday motorists to exercise caution and patience to reduce the appalling holiday traffic death toll. And he urged Americans to wipe out "bitter prejudice" based on "differences in skin pigmentation." He concluded: "Christmas . . . impels us to test the sincerity of our own dedication to the ideals so beautifully expressed in the Christian ethic. We are led to self-examination. . . . As we look into the mirror of conscience, we see blots and blemishes that mar the picture of a nation of people who devoutly believe that they were created in the image of their Maker."

In 1956, shortly after the crises in the Suez and in Hungary, Eisenhower told his nationwide audience:

"In this Nation's capital city we are joined tonight with millions in all our forty-eight States, and, indeed, throughout the world, in the happiness and in the hope that Christmas brings.

"Not that everyone is filled with happiness and hope in this season of rejoicing. Far from it. There is weariness—there is suffering for multitudes. There is hunger as well as happiness, slavery as well as freedom in the world tonight. But in the myriads of Christmas candles we see the vision of a better world for all people.

"In the light of Christmas, the dark curtains of the world are drawn aside for the moment. We see more clearly our neighbors next door; and our neighbors in other nations. We see ourselves and the responsibilities that belong to us. Inspired by the story of Christmas we seek to give of our happiness and abundance to others less fortunate. Even now the American people, on the farm and in the city, rallying through the Red Cross and other voluntary agencies to meet the needs of our neighbors in Hungary, are true to the spirit of Christmas."

Returning to his gentle, homiletic tone, the President concluded: "In the warm glow of the Christmas tree, it is easy to say these things, but when the trees come down and the lights are put away—as they always are—then we have a true testing of the spirit. That testing will be answered, throughout the year ahead, by the success each of us experiences in keeping alive the inspiration and exaltation of this moment.

"We must proceed by faith, knowing the light of Christmas is eternal, though we cannot always see it."

Eisenhower liked to issue special Christmas messages to such groups as the Boy Scouts, the U.S. Armed Forces, those in the merchant marine. In 1955 he sent a Christmas message to the people of Eastern Europe.

John F. Kennedy delivered only two Christmas messages. Eschewing the preaching or explicitly religious tone, Mr. Kennedy approached the tree-lighting ceremony as "an important responsibility," "a formal way of initiating the Christmas season."

In 1962 he noted how widespread the practice of Christmas celebrations had become. "We mark the festival of Christmas which is the most sacred and hopeful day in our civilization. For nearly 2,000 years the message of Christmas, the message of peace and goodwill towards all men, has been the guiding star of our endeavors. This morning I had a meeting at the White House which included some of our representatives from far-off countries in Africa and Asia. They were returning to their posts for the Christmas holidays. Talking with them afterwards, I was struck by the fact that in the far-off continents Moslems, Hindus, Buddhists, as well as Christians, pause from their labors on the 25th day of December to celebrate the birthday of the Prince of Peace. There could be no more striking proof that Christmas is truly the universal holiday of all men. It is the day when all of us dedicate our thoughts to others; when all are reminded that mercy and compassion are the enduring virtues; when all show, by small deeds and large and by acts, that it is more blessed to give than to receive."

In 1961, President Kennedy told West Berliners in a special Christmas message that the "beacon of freedom in Berlin will continue to shine brightly for many years to come. We are at your side as before and we shall stay. Until truly there is goodwill among

117

*Lyndon Johnson shares a moment with his
family before the tree-lighting ceremony*

men, not walls to divide them, our pursuit of peace shall continue."

Lyndon Johnson, Richard Nixon, and Gerald Ford opted for low-key Christmas messages that tended to link the fortune of the nation with the spirit and mood of the holiday season.

Johnson had the sorrowful task of delivering his first Christmas remarks one month after the assassination of John Kennedy. The lighting of the Christmas tree represented the end of the thirty-day period of national mourning.

Mr. Johnson said: "Tonight we come to the end of the season

118

of great national sorrow, and to the beginning of the season of great, eternal joy. We mourn our great President, John F. Kennedy, but he would have us go on. While our spirits cannot be light, our hearts need not be heavy.

"We were taught by Him whose birth we commemorate that after death there is life. We can believe, and we do believe, that from the death of our national leader will come a rebirth of the finest qualities of our national life.

"We have our faults and we have our failings, as any mortal society must. But when sorrow befell us, we learned anew how great is the trust and how close is the kinship that mankind feels for us, and most of all, that we feel for each other. We must remember, and we must never forget, that the hopes and the fears of all the years rest with us, as with no other people in all history. We shall keep that trust working, as always we have worked, for peace on earth and good will among men."

Richard Nixon emphasized America's contributions to peace and good will and celebrated its achievements as a nation in his seasonal remarks. Peace was the touchstone of his 1969 address. He said: "But above everything else in this Christmas season, as we open this Pageant of Peace and as we light this Nation's Christmas tree, our wish, our prayer, is for peace, the kind of peace that we can live with, the kind of peace that we can be proud of, the kind of peace that exists not just for now but that gives a chance for our children also to live in peace.

"That is what we believe in. That is what Americans stand for and that, believe me, is what we shall have.

"And, my friends, I also say to you that as we look at this great tree, there is an old saying about Christmas trees. It goes something like this: May a Christmas tree be as sturdy as faith, as high as hope, as wide as love. And I could add, may a Christmas tree, our Christmas tree, be as beautiful as peace.

"I think it is. I think it will be. And may this moment be one that history will record was one in which America looked forward to a decade of the seventies in which we could celebrate our Christmases at peace with all the world."

Gerald Ford returned to the Hoover tradition of brief, understated messages. In 1974, for example, he said: "Mrs. Ford and I send our warmest holiday greetings to all our fellow citizens. We hope that each of you will share the traditional joys of this Holy season with your family and friends. And we pray that the Christ-

President and Mrs. Reagan at their family Christmas tree in the living quarters at the White House

mas spirit of generosity and renewal will be with you throughout the coming year.

"We begin 1975 in the midst of many serious challenges. As we work to resolve them, let us be encouraged by counting the blessings we have gained from those who have met similar challenges in the past. Let us draw strength from our unity of purpose and hope from our past resourcefulness. And let us work together to ensure that the good which we have achieved will be strengthed and preserved for our children and future generations."

Jimmy Carter, one of our most personally religious presidents, preferred the simple, direct touch. In 1979 he alluded to the hostage crisis, talked about nuclear disarmament, the pope's recent visit, and the Year of the Child. At the President's direction, the lights on the fifty small trees were to remain unlighted until, the President said, "the American hostages come home." Only the "Star of Hope on the top of the great Christmas tree" was lighted. It was that year, also, that Mr. Carter lighted a menorah in Lafayette Park to honor the Jewish festival of Hanukkah.

Carter reminded his audience that year: "Christmas means a lot of things. It means love. It means warmth. It means friendship. It means family. It means joy. It means light. But everyone this Christmas will not be experiencing those deep feelings. At this moment there are fifty Americans who don't have freedom, who don't have joy, and who don't have warmth, who don't have their families with them. And there are fifty American families in this Nation who also will not experience all the joys and the light and the happiness of Christmas."

Ronald Reagan's 1981 address ranks with the messages of Roosevelt and Truman for its eloquence and warmth. He immediately made Americans feel that he was honored to be their servant. Then he spoke movingly of the meaning of Christmas. Here are some highlights: "At Christmas time every home takes on a special beauty, a special warmth. That is certainly true of the White House, where so many famous Americans have spent their Christmases over the years. This fine, old home—the people's house—has seen so much, been so much a part of all our lives and history. It has been humbling and inspiring for Nancy and me to be spending our first Christmas in this place.

"We've lived here as your tenants for almost a year now. And what a year it's been. As a people, we've been through quite a lot, moments of joy, of tragedy, and of real achievement—moments that I believe have brought us all closer together.

"G. K. Chesterton once said that the world would never starve for wonders, but only for the want of wonder. At this special time of year we all renew our sense of wonder in recalling the story of the first Christmas in Bethlehem nearly two thousand years ago.

"Some celebrate Christmas as the birthday of a great and good philosopher and teacher. Others of us believe in the divinity of the Child born in Bethlehem; that He was and is the promised Prince of Peace."

The President continued in the same vein: "Tonight, in millions of American homes, the glow of the Christmas tree is a reflection of the love Jesus taught us.

"Like the shepherds and wise men of that first Christmas, we Americans have always tried to follow a higher light, a star, if you will. At lonely campfire vigils along the frontier, in the darkest days of the Great Depression, through war and peace, the twin beacons of faith and freedom have brightened the American sky. At times our footsteps may have faltered, but trusting to God's help we have never lost our way.

"Just across the way from the White House stand the two great emblems of the holiday season—a menorah, symbolizing the Jewish festival of Hanukkah, and the National Christmas Tree, a beautiful towering blue spruce from Pennsylvania."

Turning to a more somber subject, the President castigated the Soviet Union for its repression of the spirit of freedom in Poland, "a proud and ancient nation, a land of deep religious faith where Christmas has been celebrated for a thousand years."

Mr. Reagan requested that all Americans burn a lighted candle in their windows to demonstrate solidarity with the Polish people. He said: "Let the light of millions of candles in American homes give notice that the light of freedom is not going to be extinguished. We are blessed with a freedom and abundance denied to so many. Let those candles remind us that these blessings bring with them a solemn obligation—an obligation to the God who guides us, an obligation to the heritage of liberty and dignity handed down to us by our forefathers, and an obligation to the children of the world, whose future will be shaped by the way we live our lives today."

It seems fitting to end this chapter, and this book, by returning to our first President, George Washington. As a young man, he penned a charming poem which he called "On Christmas Day." He is our only President to have written a poem about Christmas. Here it is:

Assist me, Muse divine! to Sing the Morn,
On which the Saviour of Mankind was born;
But oh! what Numbers to the Theme can rise?
Unless kind Angels aid me from the Skies!
Methinks I see the tunefull Host descend,

122

And with officious Joy the Scene attend!
Hark, by their Hymns directed on the Road,
The Gladsome Shepherds find the nascent God!
And view the Infant conscious of his Birth,
Smiling bespeak Salvation to the Earth!

Bibliography

I have used the following books and signed periodical and newspaper articles.

Bailey, Olive. *Christmas with the Washingtons.* Dietz Press, 1948.

Barnett, James. *The American Christmas.* Oxford University Press, 1954.

Bishop, Jim. *FDR's Last Year.* William Morrow & Co., 1974.

Boyd, Julian P. *The Spirit of Christmas at Monticello.* Oxford University Press, 1964.

"Carters Say Farewell to White House," *U.S. News & World Report,* Dec. 28, 1980.

Coleman, Edna M. *White House Gossip from Andrew Johnson to Calvin Coolidge.* Doubleday, Page & Co., 1927.

Craig, Barbara. "Saving the White House Tree," *Des Moines Register,* Dec. 19, 1975.

Crook, Col. William H. *Through Five Administrations.* Harper & Brothers, 1910.

Delano, Mrs. James S. "Recollections of the Home Life of Abraham Lincoln," *Washington Star,* Feb. 7, 1915.

Fairfax, Beatrice. "White House Storeroom Bulges with Gifts Selected by First Lady of Land," *Washington Times Herald,* Dec. 16, 1934.

Fields, Alonzo. *My Twenty-one Years in the White House.* Coward-McCann, 1960.

Foley, Daniel J. *The Christmas Tree.* Chilton Co., 1960.

Ford, Betty, and Chase, Chris. *The Times of My Life.* Harper & Row, 1978.

Grayson, Cary T. *Woodrow Wilson: An Intimate Memoir.* Holt, Rinehart & Winston, 1960.

Heinl, Robert Debs, Jr. "Twas the Night Before Christmas . . . ," *American Heritage,* Vol. 22, No. 1 (1970), pp. 105–109.

Hogan, E. Pendleton, "Christmas at the White House," *American Motorist,* Dec. 1932.

Johnson, Mrs. Lyndon Baines. "Christmas Memories from the White House," *Redbook,* Dec. 1977.

_____. *A White House Diary.* Holt, Rinehart & Winston, 1970.

Kane, Harnett. *The Southern Christmas Book.* David McKay Co., 1958.

Keyes, Frances Parkinson. *Capital Kaleidoscope: The Story of a Washing-ton Hostess.* Harper & Brothers, 1937.

Knebel, Fletcher. "The Story of the Presidents at Christmas," *Look,* Dec. 21, 1963.

Lathem, Edward Connery (ed.). *Meet Calvin Coolidge: The Man Behind the Myth.* Stephen Greene Press, 1960.

Leech, Margaret. *In the Days of McKinley.* Harper & Brothers, 1959.

Leighton, Frances Spatz. "Christmas Traditions at the White House." American Greetings Corp.

Mazzeo, Carolyn J. "The Roosevelt Family Christmas 1898–1918." A paper prepared for the Sagamore Hill National Historic Site, 1978.

McAdoo, Eleanor Wilson, and Gaffey, Margaret. *The Woodrow Wilsons.* Macmillan Co., 1937.

Moore, Virginia. *The Madisons.* McGraw-Hill Book Co., 1979.

Nesbitt, Henrietta. *White House Diary.* Doubleday & Co., 1948.

O'Brien, Robert Lincoln. "Last Christmas at the White House," *Ladies' Home Journal* 21 (Dec. 1903).

Paddock, Charles L. "The White House at Christmas Time," *The Chris-tian Advocate,* Dec. 17, 1931.

Parks, Lillian Rogers. *My Thirty Years Backstairs at the White House.* Fleet Publishing Corp., 1961.

Pearson, Drew. "Christmas in the White House," *Redbook,* Jan. 1936.

———. "White House Lacks Yule Gayety," *Washington Post,* Dec. 25, 1962.

Perkins, Frances. *The Roosevelt I Knew.* Viking Press, 1946.

Pollack, W. G. "Christmas with Our Presidents," *Christmas,* Vol. 12 (1942).

Randall, Ruth Painter. *Lincoln's Sons.* Little, Brown & Co., 1955.

Robertson, Nan. "Children Savor White House Christmas Parties," *New York Times,* Dec. 20, 1968.

Roosevelt, Eleanor. *Eleanor Roosevelt's Christmas Book.* Dodd, Mead & Co., 1963.

Roosevelt, Elliott. *As He Saw It.* Duell, Sloan & Pearce, 1946.

Roosevelt, Theodore. *All in the Family.* G. P. Putnam's Sons, 1929.

———. *Letters to His Children.* Charles Scribner's Sons, 1919.

Ross, Ishbel. *First Lady of the South: The Life of Mrs. Jefferson Davis.* Harper & Brothers, 1958.

———. *The General's Wife: The Life of Mrs. Ulysses S. Grant.* Dodd, Mead & Co., 1959.

———. *Grace Coolidge and Her Era.* Dodd, Mead & Co., 1962.

Seager, Robert. *And Tyler Too: A Biography of John and Julia Gardiner Tyler.* McGraw-Hill Book Co., 1963.

Singleton, Esther. *The Story of the White House.* McClure Co., 1907.

Smith, Ira R. T. *Dear Mr. President.* Julian Messner, 1949.

Smith, Marie. *Entertaining in the White House.* Acropolis Books, 1967.

———. "Pat Brings Exiled Sconces Back for Christmas," *Washington Post,* Dec. 16, 1969.

Smith, Scottie Fitzgerald. "Christmas Radiance at the White House," *House & Garden,* Dec. 1967.

Snyder, Harold. Unpublished memoirs of the National Community Christmas Tree History 1923–1970. File Box 5516, Washingtoniana Archives, Martin Luther King Public Library, Washington, D.C.

Snyder, Phillip V. *The Christmas Tree Book.* Viking Press, 1976.

Thomson, Peggy. "They Made It a Capital Christmas in 1853," *Potomac,* Nov. 28, 1968.

Truman, Margaret. *Souvenir.* McGraw-Hill Book Co., 1956.

Whitney, Janet. *Abigail Adams.* Little, Brown & Co., 1947.

Wilcox, Mary Emily Donelson. *Christmas Under Three Flags.* Neale Co., 1900.

Williams, Charles Richard (ed.). *Diary and Letters of Rutherford B. Hayes, Nineteenth President of the United States,* Vol. III, 1865–1881. Columbus: The Ohio State Archaeological and Historical Society, 1924.

Wilson, Edith Bolling. *My Memoir.* Bobbs-Merrill Co., 1939.

Young, J. Russell. "Roosevelt's Christmas Mail Breaks White House Records," *Washington Star,* Dec. 22, 1933.

I have also used *The New York Times* extensively, beginning with 1906. The references from 1906 to 1981 are too numerous to list. In addition, I consulted the *New York Tribune* from 1880 to 1908, the *Washington Star* in 1879, 1890, 1917, 1929, and 1934, and *The Washington Post* for 1952, 1962, and 1972–1981, inclusive.